Writing With Your HEAD & Your HEART

Balancing Logic and Emotion to Create Powerful Nonfiction

JAMES J. LOMUSCIO

Norwalk Community College
Western Connecticut State University

Boston   Burr Ridge, IL   Dubuque, IA   New York   San Francisco   St. Louis
Bangkok   Bogotá   Caracas   Lisbon   London   Madrid
Mexico City   Milan   New Delhi   Seoul   Singapore   Sydney   Taipei   Toronto

The **McGraw·Hill** Companies

Writing With Your HEAD & Your HEART
Balancing Logic and Emotion to Create Powerful Nonfiction

1 2 3 4 5 6 7 8 9 0 BLA BLA 0 9 8

ISBN-13: 978-0-07-353840-X
ISBN-10: 0-07-353840-2

Learning Solutions Specialist: Tom Weitz
Production Editor: Nicole Baumgartner
Cover Design: Dylan Breton
Printer/Binder: Perfect Printing

WRITING WITH YOUR HEAD AND YOUR HEART:

Balancing Logic and Emotion to Create Powerful Nonfiction

BY

JAMES J. LOMUSCIO

This book is dedicated to all my students, past and present, at Norwalk Community College and Western Connecticut State University. Their writings have opened up new worlds to me, worlds that would have remained closed and forgotten if not for the need to write.

It is also for my Mother, who instilled in me the love of good story, and for my wife Christine, who urged me to write this book. Both remain my staunchest critics.

It's none of their business that you have to learn to write. Let them think you were born that way.

—Ernest Hemingway

Table of Contents

Introduction

Your Life, Your View, Your Words

As I walk into class at the start of each semester, I see new faces, many of them smiling nervously about a course they have long dreaded. Though this is a college freshman course, some of the students are sophomores, juniors and on rare occasions, seniors. The latter have obviously put off the inevitable for as long as they could before having to face this class required to graduate.

The course goes by many names at different institutions: "English Composition," "The Habit of Writing," "Rhetoric," "Basic Composition," "Academic Writing," and "College Writing." Whatever the nomenclature, the purpose is the same—for students to write and to write well.

This course asks you to do what society expects of someone who is the product of higher education: to ask questions, to seek out answers, to research, to think critically, to incorporate your own opinions, to articulate your thoughts with confidence, to write them down in an interesting and compelling fashion, to establish credibility and authority—to ultimately contribute to civilization's collective body of knowledge. Sounds lofty for a freshman comp course, right? But that's the goal.

You will achieve this goal by writing, rewriting and writing again to craft polished nonfiction that includes opinion pieces, observations, interviews, analyses, reviews, and research papers to be shared with an educated adult audience.

Each semester, whether I'm teaching traditional college-age students or adults taking evening classes, the writing curve is about the same.

There are the lucky few who have been told that they have a talent for writing, and thus possess a smoldering passion for the written word. It's a raw talent, an ability they need to refine, rework, and refine again to create the best possible prose. Freshman composition will be a time of validation and growth for them. Some may even become tomorrow's professional writers.

1

Most college students, however, teenagers and adults alike, arrive with a sense of dread. Some may even have phobias about writing. They might even feel the walls closing in, and perhaps will need to excuse themselves. Why? Because unlike math, scientific data and courses dependent upon single answers or multiple choice tests, writing, no matter how technical the subject matter might be, requires students to present part of themselves. The act requires them to bare part of their souls no matter how impersonal and technical the subject may be.

In short, writing puts you on the spot because you have to face yourself first. Ergo, it's no wonder writing assignments, and this is no flippant exaggeration nor hyperbole, rank up there with the likes of paying bills, doing one's income taxes, even root canal surgery. Writing truly scares some people, and procrastination reigns as the flawed solution.

As an author and someone who's spent nearly 30 years writing and editing for newspapers and magazines, I'm always baffled by such fear. I equate writing with breathing. Why does it make others feel as if they are drowning? What turns off some individuals from exercising such a basic life skill, irreconcilably so? I don't mean to sound grandiose, but a writing class is a sacred opportunity to express oneself in a way nobody ever has, nor will. It's a chance to add your view of the world to all that's gone before you.

Isn't it odd that such a basic right of self expression, one that's protected by the Constitution, seems so daunting to so many? Was it all the red ink of elementary, middle, and secondary school that left indelible marks? Did strict grammarians make them feel inept, disregarding students' theses for commas when new writers in need of nurturing dared to share their thoughts? Or maybe it was a move in the other direction. Perhaps some teachers in well intentioned attempts not to scare them off coddled students to the point of relativism. That is, if all writing is acceptable, none of it really holds any value.

But it does. Words have more power than you can imagine. Our very nation and civilizations throughout history sprung from and were forged by ideas fashioned into words—words that inspired, motivated, comforted and called others to action for humanity's betterment.

As I poll a new class to plumb the depths of students' fears, I hear these standard responses:

"I've never been good at writing."

"I have a problem with grammar, run-ons and being repetitive."

"English is my second language, and it never comes out the way I mean to say it."

"I can't get it from my head to the paper."

"I have problems with organization."

"I run out of things to say."

"I just don't like to write."

"I hate writing."

I find the last two comments most baffling, especially when it comes from traditional college-age students, 18 to 22 year olds. You were virtually weaned on computers. You are more keyboard proficient—and thus write more—than any previous generation in human history. From text messages to emails to instant messages and so on, yours is a generation that thrives on communicating via written words. Why then such apprehension about stringing words into sentences, sentences into paragraphs and paragraphs into essays? It doesn't follow. And such barriers persist beyond college, carrying through to the business world and into the highest of corporate suites.

If you are one of these individuals or one of the few who really want to write, use this text as your guide book on a spectacular journey. To paraphrase "Star Trek," join us to boldly go where you—and no one else—have ever gone before. Show us the world, the whole universe even, through your eyes, your head, and your heart.

You'll begin your journey by breaking down barriers, eschewing past pains and fears, and discovering your own voice. As we progress, you will begin to see the craft and art of writing not a source of confusion but as a means of clarifying your life.

You will accomplish this goal by learning to write with your head and your heart, balancing logic and emotion to create powerful nonfiction.

Remember, no one else has ever seen the world exactly the way you do, and no one else ever will. Your voice counts.

Chapter One: The Seven Rules of Good Writing

Words are the most powerful drug used by mankind.

—**Rudyard Kipling**

Words have power. Used judiciously they can affect great social change and enrich countless lives. Used improperly and with malice, words can injure, maim, or kill, if not bore one to the point of feeling dead. It's unfortunate that in our culture of instant communication, there is little good writing out there.

Oh, there's a lot of writing, or what may pass for it. But let's be honest. There's plenty of boring, bogus, or poorly crafted nonfiction floating out in cyberspace or on the printed page. Call it noise, static, or keyboard catharsis. Call it a waste of ink, the untimely end of a good tree, a waste of electricity. Call it anything but good writing.

Good writing doesn't just happen. It doesn't come out of thin air or spring from a well bubbling over with creativity. Many beginning writers wish it did. They erroneously and naively believe they can tap into the right zone, an inspirational website, if your will, where perfect words will flow from a mystical source to their fingers. For new writers it doesn't happen this way. Good writing requires work, the old inspiration meets perspiration kind of work. And there are rules, not Draconian ones, but rules nonetheless.

Here are my **"Seven Rules of Good Writing."** I've often shared them with students and reporters who worked for me. Study them closely and commit to them. We will be referring to them throughout this text.

1.) You Can't Be a Good Writer Unless You Are a Good Reader.

Who would consider being a musician without listening to music? Playing basketball without ever watching a game? Fixing a car, building a house, even tying your shoes for that matter without ever watching how it is done? The answer is obviously no one.

Yet when I ask a new freshman composition class how many students read a daily newspaper or weekly magazine, I'm lucky if two hands go up. Think about it. How many other things would you do in life without studying them or watching them first? None. So when it comes to good writing remember this tongue twister: *read reputable writing regularly*—and not just required school texts.

Not only will you expose yourself to good grammar and add to your vocabulary bank. Reading good writing helps you develop a sense of how a main point, the thesis, is presented and developed. You get to see how good stories and essays are organized and flow seamlessly from beginning to end. The good writing of others is a valuable roadmap to use in finding your own voice.

2.) Good Writing is the Result of Good Thinking.

Ever talk to someone who rambles, never gets to the point, or goes off on tangents? If you are not looking at your watch, there's a good chance you have begun to think about other things. This speaker loses his or her listener because he or she speaks without thinking about what is being said. They are out of touch with their listeners, their audience. It is even worse when such rambling occurs in writing. Individuals like this are too involved with themselves and overcome with emotion and distractions to tell a story in any logical order. Good writing, like good thinking, demands a point, which again is called your thesis in academia. It also requires organization, sequence and flow. Note that when writing is the result of good thinking, you will leave the reader thinking, too.

3.) Good Writing Requires a Balance of Logic and Emotion.

This is where the head and the heart come into play. Again, think about your audience. You are writing for an audience of humans, not supercomputers—and humans are emotional as well as intelligent beings. You must strive to relate to the audience on a human level.

Even Albert Einstein's Nobel Prize winning "Theory of Relativity" speaks to us on a personal level. In a section on space and time, he describes traveling on a train, dropping a stone on the embankment and a pedestrian observing the misdeed.

"The purpose of mechanics is to describe how bodies change their position in space and 'time'," he writes. "I should load my conscience with grave sins against the sacred spirit of lucidity were I to formulate the aims of mechanics in this way, without serious reflections and detailed explanations. Let us proceed to disclose these sins."

Not quite the egg head, techno-speak you would expect from one of the world's greatest scientists. In fact, Einstein uses religious symbolism to make an emotional connection, as well as describing something mundane many can relate to, riding on a train. As a result, his brainy treatise becomes more accessible than you would expect.

Remember, if there's too much logic at the expense of a human connection, your readers will feel detached and become easily bored.

Conversely, if there's too much emotion, you will forfeit your credibility. If your opinion piece on affordable housing, illegal immigration, and escalating gasoline prices gets too emotional, your logic will suffer—and what might have been a powerful, persuasive argument ends up sounding like some guy ranting from a bar stool. People usually tune them out.

Remember, the right balance between logic and emotion is critical to good writing.

4.) Good Writing Requires Good Character.

When it comes to writing nonfiction, credibility is everything. James Frey, author of "A Million Little Pieces" learned that the hard way when it was discovered he had fabricated a number of pages in his so-called true memoir. Jason Blair, the infamous reporter for the *New York Times* who made up stories he had never covered, learned this truth the hard way, too. The *Times* booted him from what might have been a promising career. Janet Cook of the *Washington Post* even lost the Pulitzer Prize along with her job when it was learned she had fabricated a powerful, well written story about a young boy she claimed was a heroin addict.

These three were individuals who altered the truth as they tried to make facts fit the story they wanted to write. That may be fine in fiction, but in nonfiction it's the gravest of crimes. That's because when you lose your credibility, your word, you lose everything. All authority, a word in which the first seven letters spell "author", is gone. As an author of nonfiction, you must revere the truth.

In addition to balanced logic and emotion, powerful nonfiction requires ethics, something the ancient Greeks called ethos. Let this triad of *logos* (literally word and used to denote logic), *pathos* (emotion) and *ethos* guide all of your writing.

Ethics, of course, requires more than just telling the truth. It involves a pact you will make with yourself to avoid plagiarism, to respect another's intellectual property and to give credit where credit is due by using proper attributions, in-text citations and a "Works Cited" page. In an age of cut and paste and term papers for sale on the internet, the need for ethics and character among writers has never been greater.

5.) Good Writing Demands Showing, not Just Telling.

I know, by now you are probably thinking that line is so cliché, something you have probably heard writing teachers preach since you were in grammar school. But just because it is an often repeated line does not diminish its importance. As a subway straphanger (the guy who couldn't find a seat) years back, I spied an advertisement for the New York Daily News I never forgot. It stated, "Our words are worth a thousand pictures." That stuck with me because the old saw, "A picture is worth a thousand words," seemed to have been heralding the end of the written word, i.e. newspapers, to electronic media. It never happened. That's because words can do so much more than pictures ever could.

Through examples, images, metaphors and similes, words can pierce us, become imprinted on our mind's eye, leaving an image we will never forget. Consider these lines penned by Dr. Martin Luther King in his *Letter from a Birmingham Jail*:

"Perhaps it is easy for those who have never felt the stinging darts of segregation to say, 'Wait.' But when you see the vicious mobs lynch your mothers and father at will and drown your sisters and brothers at whim; when you have seen hate-filled policemen curse, kick, and even kill your black brothers and sisters; when you see the vast majority of your twenty million Negro brothers smothering in an airtight cage of poverty in the midst of an affluent society. . . then you will understand why we find it difficult to wait."

These words possess tremendous power because they vividly show the plight of African-American in pre-civil rights America. It was this type of prose rich with images that moved others to affect great social change.

6.) Good Writing Must Be Clear and Concise.

*The most valuable of all talents is that of never using
two words when one will do.*

—**Thomas Jefferson**

They call it an economy of words, and as someone who cut his teeth in a newsroom, I saw the economy of words literally. Long-winded sentences and unnecessary words cost ink, newsprint, even ad space. It's no wonder that the old hunt-and-peck newshounds had to choose their words carefully.

I once remember an editor saying that each word you write will cost you a nickel and that you have only been given so many nickels to write a story. "Can you really afford to waste that many nickels?" I heard him yell at one writer. So, maybe you shouldn't buy that extra adjective or adverb. Try a stronger verb or noun. Look at the following sentence, for example.

"Two city men, who had been attempting to flee the rapidly rising waters in downtown Essex caused by the overflowing river due to five days of non-stop rain, were swept into the Connecticut River and later pulled to safety two miles away by a police helicopter."

I guess it's grammatically passable, but it's painful. That's 46 words. The writer is saying too much. Beyond costing $2.30 in nickels, it's costing the reader's attention. A clearer, more concise way of writing it would be:

"A police chopper safely pulled two Essex men from the Connecticut River after floodwaters from five-day downpour swept them on a turbulent, two-mile ride."

That's only 24 words, or just $1.20, and it conveys the same information without weighing us down with excess verbiage. Think frugally. Use your imaginary nickels to buy the best words. Don't say something in seven words if you can say it in two or three. Don't waste words on the obvious.

By being concise, you will add to the clarity of what you want to say. You won't be tempted to muddy your prose with jargon, psychobabble and euphemisms. Not to be insensitive, but the word "die" is more direct than "to pass away." While the military may call them "anti-personnel devices" to the rest of us they are called "bombs." And lines like, "She is a kind and caring person who knows how to really relate to others because she is centered and has a good self image," make us cringe. Shrouded in such pretentious language, this line tells us nothing. You would be better off giving examples of how this person is good to others. When you waste words with empty blather, you bore the reader.

You can also bore – or lose – the reader by hiding behind what I like to call fifty-cent, polysyllabic words. Some beginning writers feel they have to impress the reader with such grandiose, highfalutin vocabulary. They think it will make them sound important, educated. While every word has its place, even fifty-cent words, remember that the main purpose of language is to communicate, not make your readers constantly run to the dictionary. In short, use impressive words only when they are the best word to describe what you want to say, and always consider the audience. Don't use language that will confuse, muddy, or obfuscate (How's that for a fifty-cent word?) the point you want to make. Use words that will best explain what you want to say, even if such words cost but a mere nickel.

I recall a press conference interview years ago with the late William F. Buckley, Jr. He answered my question all right, but I must admit he was hard to follow. His response almost seemed cryptic. It's no surprise that upon Mr. Buckley's death, the New York Times, in their headline, no less, referred to him as "Sesquipedalian." Now that's a ten-dollar word. Merriam-Webster defines it as given to or characterized by the use of long words. The Times seemed to have fun with the headline. That word was Mr. Buckley to a tee.

Besides those who use expensive words, writing's biggest spendthrifts are those given to redundancies. I jokingly tell students that just because I may have liked something stated in the third paragraph doesn't mean I'll want to hear it again in the fourth and fifth paragraphs. Never pad your writing to make a word count. And avoid all fillers and artificial ingredients. Padding a composition only proves that you're bored writing the piece. And if you're bored writing an essay, imagine how the reader will feel.

7.) The Secret of Writing is in the Rewriting.

Books aren't written, they're rewritten. . . . It is one of the hardest things to accept, especially after the seventh rewrite hasn't quite done it. . .
— **Michael Crichton**

Half my life is an act of revision.
— **John Irving**

A lot of beginning writers become discouraged because they don't get it right the first time. I can't think of one professional writer who gets it perfect on the first try. Think about it. If all writers were in the habit of cranking out great prose from the start, it would take a heavy toll on the economy. Never mind the fact that the rubber industry would suffer substantial losses since the need for erasers would plummet. Or the fact that Wite-Out would never have been invented, nor correcting typewriter ribbons, nor delete keys on computer keyboards. Paper companies would take a huge hit, too, since scrap paper and hard copy revisions would be superfluous. And that doesn't even begin to consider the impact on the publishing industry. Many editors, be they fact checkers or copyeditors, and writers, including ghostwriters, would be out of work. There would be no need for college composition courses, or, *gasp*, textbooks to go with them. In short, to err with your first, second, even third draft is human. To revise a piece of writing into the best prose possible can be a divine experience.

Examine the following example of obviously unedited prose.

"So he took the fifteen thousand dollars. My lawyer is haveing prostrate gland trouble in Philadelphia and his assistant lawyer doesn't know his prostrate from a hole in the ground so I haveing heard from them yet. But if the law still same as it was pieces contracted to write by a bona-fide non-resident written while out of the country are tax free if non-resident out of the country over six consecutive months. Maybe now it is changed but if my prostrated lawyers find that is so I can give the monies back or just write the piece and the stories and take the loss same as always."

Where do we start? Misplaced periods? Prostrate instead of prostate? Run-ons? The glaring misspelling, "haveing?" Making no sense? Such writing is an instructor's nightmare. If it happens on an in-class final essay, the student would most likely fail.

Oddly enough, these words were written by one of America's greatest literary icons—Ernest Hemingway—in a letter sent from De Paula, Cuba on June 27, 1948 to his friend and biographer A.E. Hotchner. Hotchner reprinted the letter in his book, *Dear Papa, Dear Hotch: The Correspondence of Ernest Hemingway and A.E. Hotchner*. Note that Hemingway had already been established as one of our nation's preeminent authors at the time of this letter.

How could this be? Some speculate that Hemingway didn't care because the letter was never meant to be published. Or that he had too much to drink. That he was just being sloppy. Or that this great American writer really needed good editors.

I cite this passage to show that no writers, no matter how elevated, are beyond reproach. All of us can and do make errors, and the secret of writing lies in rewriting. That means stepping away from your work and viewing it objectively, as a reader. It also means making the necessary changes.

Some beginning writers, those who realize they have talent, are not as amenable to editing, either from themselves or others. To them, their words are golden, and any editing would be a desecration akin to putting a moustache on the Mona Lisa. Why mess with perfection?

Unfortunately, their prose is far from perfect. These kinds of writers, if they ever make it to a publication, are an editor's worst nightmare, and they don't last long in the profession.

That's not to say that you shouldn't stand up for your work, or that you can't negotiate with editors be they professionals or your classroom peer editors. But good writing requires that you be open minded when it comes to criticism, that you value the importance of the rewrite, and that you understand your drafts are works in progress. In fact, everything you write this semester barring your final polished draft will be a work in progress, so don't shun improvements.

Understand that freshman composition is as much about the process as it is about the product. Professional writers go through this every day, whether they are researching and writing stories for the *New York Times*, writing a chapter for a new book, or penning lines of poetry. I recall a writers' workshop on Block Island, Rhode Island one summer. I met a poet in the morning, and by the time I saw her again in the afternoon, she said she had the most productive day. She had written two lines.

Of course freshman composition, prose as opposed to poetry, will garner much a greater turnout at a better rate. The point is that words and ideas are a lot like potter's clay. We have to keep shaping, forming, and massaging them to create the best possible work worthy of showcasing.

You're aim is to make your writing the best it can possibly be because it represents you. It even bears your name.

Assignments:

1.) Read several different newspapers each day over the next week. Choose an eclectic mix, from well-respected ones such as the Wall Street Journal, the New York Times, the Washington Post, and USA Today to your local community newspapers whether weekly or daily publications, to even the supermarket tabloids. Study the writing in each? Which ones have the most credibility? Which writing style do you prefer? Which one best uses economy of words? Which paper and story offers the right balance of logic and emotion?

2.) Do the same with several different magazines from Time and Newsweek to Esquire, Cosmopolitan to People. Again, which writing styles do you prefer? Which authors seemed to show the most authority and credibility? Give examples of authors who showed examples and made their stories come alive as opposed to merely telling.

3.) Based upon what you have learned in "The Seven Rules of Good Writing," write an imaginary letter to Ernest Hemingway explaining why he must go back and redo his letter.

4.) Write a two-page paper as to why you believe many people today are ill at ease about writing compositions. Use your own experiences and those of classmates willing to share their experiences.

Chapter Two: Through Your Unique Lens

My aim is to put down what I see and
what I feel in the best and simplest way I can tell it.

—**Ernest Hemingway**

We all view the world through our own lens. Our perceptions are unique. They're ours.

Nobody, not even two reporters asked to cover the same event as objectively as possible can escape their own subjectivity. Sure, they may strive for objectivity, unbiased coverage, in their quest for the truth. But their subjectivity, that is, their viewpoint, will always impact it depending upon myriad factors including their age, height, weight, gender, eyesight, and location in time and space. If it sounds complicated, consider this example.

As an editor I send out two reporters to cover the exact same car accident on the Post Road. Both reporters get the names of the victims, the fact that one had to be taken to the hospital for minor injuries, the speed at which they were going, the makes and years of the cars. In short, they get the typical 5Ws: who, what, when, where, and why. For what it's worth, I have two stories that are basically the same.

However, one reporter, from where she was standing, caught the glimmer of sunshine on the mangled, crumpled, chrome side view mirror. She adds that description to her story. She also adds the designer name of the female victim's handbag, a Coach pocketbook, that she saw the paramedic retrieve and carry into the ambulance. While observing, she overheard the paramedic say to check the bag for the woman's "heart meds."

The other reporter, because of his keen hearing, notices falling drops of green anti-freeze from the Lexus SUV's smashed radiator. And from where he is standing his discerns more than 20 feet of skid marks made by the SUV before it rammed the side of a Mercedes. Having grown up in a home with a diesel powered Mercedes, he incorporates the smell of diesel fuel into his story, too.

Other than these differences, the stories are pretty much the same because these writers, in traditional, Associated Press style journalism, strove for objectivity. Still, their unique selves came through. Each view is important, which is why informed individuals always want to read more than one account of an event. It's as if everyone has a specific piece of one great truth.

Your unique self really shines through when instead of trying to be as objective as possible, you embrace your subjectivity, your views, in an essay. Unlike straight forward news stories, essays are designed to welcome your point of view, your thesis.

Writing an essay by observing is a great way to blend objectivity and subjectivity. Sure, you will report what you see, but you will also use your mind's eye to draw comparisons, analogies, and metaphors as only you can. Again, your view counts, and the reader gets to view the world through your eyes.

Take a look at the following example. We'll call it "The Fan."

It was a sweltering early September evening in a Stamford, Connecticut ENG 101 classroom without air-conditioning, and it was hard to concentrate, not the best way to begin a new semester. The students and I, our shirts saturated with perspiration, vainly sought relief fanning ourselves with manila folders, binders, or anything else that could move air. It wasn't long before I retrieved an oscillating fan from another classroom. It was a rickety old thing about a foot high, and it had three speeds, fast, faster and too fast to use lest it catch fire. The fan would have to do, and I positioned it on a front desk.

The welcome breezes mesmerized the class, a diverse mix of traditional college-age students and adults, many of them foreign students. They stared at the fan as if in homage. I saw it as the perfect opportunity to assign an in-class observation essay.

"Write about the fan, and tell me what you see," I instructed them. "Write with your eyes, all of your senses, even your imagination."

They were surprisingly motivated, and the resulting, brief, handwritten essays proved without a doubt that everyone has something interesting to say.

One middle-aged woman from Haiti described the way she felt when the fan turned in her direction. She imagined being caressed by balmy Caribbean breezes on her native beach.

A Midwestern man who worked for local manufacturer was much more technical in his description. He timed the oscillations. He homed in on the fan's chrome grill work. He even described a faint cranking sound as the fan swept from left to right.

Even a young man with a tough guy attitude, his tattooed arms folded, a pack of cigarettes rolled high in his sleeve, got into the assignment. He wrote:

"It stands there alone, moving its head back and forth, nervous, like a crack dealer on the corner."

And there were other takes on this simple fan, each one as unique as the person seeing it through their eyes. All of the students read, opening up new worlds to the rest of us—all because of watching a little fan on a hot night.

Observing is key to all writing. All things, big and small, novel and mundane, are fodder for brilliant prose if you focus with your head and your heart.

Examine the following observation exercise written by Brian Coppola, a student in my Spring 2008 "Introduction to the Creative Process" class at Western Connecticut State University in Danbury. Students were asked to focus on any object or place using their eyes for details–and their mind's eye–to make their prose go beyond the obvious. Brian achieves that goal with the following essay, "Lucky Soles."

LUCKY SOLES

By Brian Coppola

The color was just about faded to a yellowish, light tan. The soles, the tips, and the siding were much lighter than they used to be. When I had bought them they were dark tan, but after hundreds of missions, thousands of miles of walking, and years of wear, the original color was no where to be found. It was as if they had been left out in the sun for days and the blazing rays just sucked the life out of them. Although they have probably been worn over a thousand times, they still felt comfortable feeling, as if I had just taken them out of the box. You can't throw something like these away. They have survived every dangerous mission with me in Iraq and have yet to fail me once. These were my lucky boots.

The shoelaces were worn out and old as well. They looked like they had been buried for years and someone just pulled them out of the ground and laced them up. Dirt spots and stripes ran up and down them like those of a zebra. The laces were a dark brownish tan color and were dirty like a person rolling around in the dust while wearing a white t-shirt. The tips where the plastic used to be were completely chewed off, so if you were ever to unlace and lace them back you would have a tough time getting them through the holes. I probably should have gotten a new pair of laces years ago, but I liked the old ones. They've been strong since the day I've bought them and they too have yet to fail me.

Besides the color being faded out, the boots were in pretty good shape. There were no major holes in them and the soles were still perfectly in tact. Almost every mark and every scratch have its own story. The biggest story of the boots was the few minor scrapes on the tip of the left boot. It looked like a cat had got a hold of it and clawed it. But it was far from a cat. It was caused by a roadside bomb in Baghdad on July 14th 2006. We hit an IED, and a piece of shrapnel came through the truck floor and just scraped the top of my boot. My friends always used to tell me how lucky I was. But I always used to tell them it was the boots.

The insides of the boots felt like the first time I ever tried them on. They still felt very comfortable and cozy. The insulation was still fresh and the lining had not been ripped at all. You would think that after slipping them on and off thousands and thousands of times they would somehow be disfigured, but they were still in perfect condition. The lining was black with a red trim around the edges. The white stitching along the outsides of the fabric still looked like railroad tracks. If it wasn't for the color and the outsides being worn out, you would think you were wearing brand new boots if you ever slipped them on.

Ever since I pulled them out of the closet I began to remember all the important missions and memories I had lived through in them. To other people they were just ordinary old, worn-out combat boots, but to me they more. To me they were the lucky boots that got me through combat and brought me home safely. They were the boots I left for war with, and they were the boots I came back to the U.S. in.

Response Assignment:

1.) Why does the writer consider the boots to be lucky?

2.) What are the most powerful images in the essay?

3.) How does the writer blend the use of recall with observation? Is it effective?

4.) What about the essay's tone and the writer's voice? How would you describe them? Are the effective in moving the writing forward?

Writing Assignments:

1.) Examine the layout and the decor of the classroom you are in, and describe it using all of your senses.

2.) Study the scene or artwork on a postage stamp and describe it in on one or two typed pages. Use your eyes, your head and your heart.

3.) Do the same with coin, perhaps one of the state commemorative quarters.

4.) Find a quiet spot in a coffee shop, diner or cafeteria and observe the scene, the people, and the action. Use all of your senses to make your prose come alive.

5.) Describe what it is like being a passenger in an automobile, a commuter train, a subway car, a cab, a hansom cab, a boat, etc. Describe the scene, the people observed, the sense of movement, change, smells, wind, and your sense of touch. Use your mind's eye, too, describing what thoughts, reminiscences and emotions are conjured up by your trip.

Chapter Three: The Big Picture

Everybody walks past a thousand story ideas every day.
The good writers are the ones who see five or six of them.
Most people don't see any.

—Orson Scott Card

If you look at anything long enough,
say just that wall in front of you—it will come out of that wall.

—Anton Chekhov

Observing is a great exercise to make you aware of the world around you, to awaken your senses. It is an invaluable tool because you cannot be a good writer unless you tune into your environs, noticing and musing about things you have often overlooked. Writers who heighten their senses and sensitivities really never stop working.

In the pulp novel, "Dirty Laundry," author Pete Hamill, a former newspaper columnist, tells the tale about a feature writer and his former girlfriend. The protagonist bemoans their incompatibility, saying that the girlfriend could never understand that a writer is working even when he's just looking out a window. In our results-based culture, this may sound like a con, the idea person who never breaks a sweat. But writers do sweat, whether working on their third drafts or foraging for ideas through observation.

It's important to note that observation is more than just recording what we see. It's a springboard for critical thinking, for looking at the big picture.

The following two writers do just that as their observations bring them to philosophize about life and death. In the first, "The Death of a Moth" by Virginia Woolf, the author uses common summer sight: a moth trapped, flapping frantically by a window, as a microcosm for life's meaning.

In the second piece, "A Hanging," author George Orwell explores the meaning of existence by examining that which we hold most sacred, human life. From the seemingly insignificant to the most significant, both authors use their skills of observation to establish important theses.

21

Read the following two essays and examine how each author uses her or his head and heart to write compelling prose. Notice how their observations are not frivolous. They are important in elevating the prose to have higher meaning.

THE DEATH OF THE MOTH
By Virginia Woolf

Moths that fly by day are not properly to be called moths; they do not excite that pleasant sense of dark autumn nights and ivy-blossom which the commonest yellow-under wing asleep in the shadow of the curtain never fails to rouse in us. They are hybrid creatures, neither gay like butterflies nor sombre like their own species. Nevertheless the present specimen, with his narrow hay-coloured wings, fringed with a tassel of the same colour, seemed to be content with life. It was a pleasant morning, mid-September, mild, benignant, yet with a keener breath than that of the summer months. The plough was already scoring the field opposite the window, and where the share had been, the earth was pressed flat and gleamed with moisture. Such vigour came rolling in from the fields and the down beyond that it was difficult to keep the eyes strictly turned upon the book. The rooks too were keeping one of their annual festivities; soaring round the tree tops until it looked as if a vast net with thousands of black knots in it had been cast up into the air; which, after a few moments sank slowly down upon the trees until every twig seemed to have a knot at the end of it. Then, suddenly, the net would be thrown into the air again in a wider circle this time, with the utmost clamour and vociferation, as though to be thrown into the air and settle slowly down upon the tree tops were a tremendously exciting experience.

The same energy which inspired the rooks, the ploughmen, the horses, and even, it seemed, the lean bare-backed downs, sent the moth fluttering from side to side of his square of the window-pane. One could not help watching him. One was, indeed, conscious of a queer feeling of pity for him. The possibilities of pleasure seemed that morning so enormous and so various that to have only a moth's part in life, and a day moth's at that, appeared a hard fate, and his zest in enjoying his meagre opportunities to the full, pathetic. He flew vigorously to one corner of his compartment, and, after waiting there a second, flew across to the other. What remained for him but to fly to a third corner and then to a fourth? That was all he could do, in spite of the size of the downs, the width of the sky, the far-off smoke of houses, and the romantic voice, now and then, of a steamer out at sea. What he could do he did. Watching him, it seemed as if a fibre, very thin but pure, of the enormous energy of the world had been thrust into his frail and diminutive body. As often as he crossed the pane, I could fancy that a thread of vital light became visible. He was little or nothing but life.

Yet, because he was so small, and so simple a form of the energy that was rolling in at the open window and driving its way through so many narrow and intricate corridors in my own brain and in those of other human beings, there was something marvelous as well as pathetic about him. It was as if someone had taken a tiny bead of pure life and decking it as lightly as possible with down and feathers, had set it dancing and zig-zagging to show us the true nature of life. Thus displayed one could not get over the strangeness of it. One is apt to forget all about life, seeing it humped and bossed and garnished and cumbered so that it has to move with the greatest circumspection and dignity. Again, the thought of all that life might have been had he been born in any other shape caused one to view his simple activities with a kind of pity.

After a time, tired by his dancing apparently, he settled on the window ledge in the sun, and, the queer spectacle being at an end, I forgot about him. Then, looking up, my eye was caught by him. He was trying to resume his dancing, but seemed either so stiff or so awkward that he could only flutter to the bottom of the window-pane; and when he tried to fly across it he failed. Being intent on other matters I watched these futile attempts for a time without thinking, unconsciously waiting for him to resume his flight, as one waits for a machine, that has stopped momentarily, to start again without considering the reason of its failure. After perhaps a seventh attempt he slipped from the wooden ledge and fell, fluttering his wings, on to his back on the window sill. The helplessness of his attitude roused me. It flashed upon me that he was in difficulties; he could no longer raise himself; his legs struggled vainly. But, as I stretched out a pencil, meaning to help him to right himself, it came over me that the failure and awkwardness were the approach of death. I laid the pencil down again.

The legs agitated themselves once more. I looked as if for the enemy against which he struggled. I looked out of doors. What had happened there? Presumably it was midday, and work in the fields had stopped. Stillness and quiet had replaced the previous animation. The birds had taken themselves off to feed in the brooks. The horses stood still.

Yet the power was there all the same, massed outside indifferent, impersonal, not attending to anything in particular. Somehow it was opposed to the little hay-coloured moth. It was useless to try to do anything. One could only watch the extraordinary efforts made by those tiny legs against an oncoming doom which could, had it chosen, have submerged an entire city, not merely a city, but masses of human beings; nothing, I knew, had any chance against death. Nevertheless after a pause of exhaustion the legs fluttered again. It was superb this last protest, and so frantic that he succeeded at last in righting himself. One's sympathies, of course, were all on the side of life. Also, when there was nobody to care or to know, this gigantic effort on the part of an insignificant little moth, against a power of such magnitude, to retain what no one else valued or desired to keep, moved one strangely. Again, somehow, one saw life, a pure bead. I lifted the pencil again, useless though I knew it to be. But even as I did so, the unmistakable tokens of death showed themselves. The body relaxed, and instantly grew stiff. The struggle was over. The insignificant little creature now knew death. As I looked at the dead moth, this minute wayside triumph of so great a force over so mean an antagonist filled me with wonder. Just as life had been strange a few minutes before, so death was now as strange. The moth having righted himself now lay most decently and uncomplainingly composed. O yes, he seemed to say, death is stronger than I am.

Response and Writing Assignments:

1.) Many people feel no emotion when they spy a dead moth or fly on a windowsill. Does Virginia Woolf make you care about this moth? Why?

2.) Where is Woolf throughout the essay? Is she inside? On the first or second floor? How does her vantage point affect what we as readers glean from her observations?

3.) Describe Woolf's observations that show life at the beginning of the essay. How does that change by the end of the essay?

4.) How does Woolf describe the moth? Are her descriptions effective? Does she show or tell? Give examples. What kinds of similes or metaphors would you have used when describing a moth beating its wings by a window in your home?

5.) What is the main point, the thesis, of the essay? Is Woolf's thesis clearly stated, or is it implied?

A HANGING

By George Orwell

It was in Burma, a sodden morning of the rains. A sickly light, like yellow tinfoil, was slanting over the high walls into the jail yard. We were waiting outside the condemned cells, a row of sheds fronted with double bars, like small animal cages. Each cell measured about ten feet by ten and was quite bare within except for a plank bed and a pot of drinking water. In some of them brown silent men were squatting at the inner bars, with their blankets draped round them. These were the condemned men, due to be hanged within the next week or two.

One prisoner had been brought out of his cell. He was a Hindu, a puny wisp of a man, with a shaven head and vague liquid eyes. He had a thick, sprouting moustache, absurdly too big for his body, rather like the moustache of a comic man on the films. Six tall Indian warders were guarding him and getting him ready for the gallows. Two of them stood by with rifles and fixed bayonets, while the others handcuffed him, passed a chain through his handcuffs and fixed it to their belts, and lashed his arms tight to his sides. They crowded very close about him, with their hands always on him in a careful, caressing grip, as though all the while feeling him to make sure he was there. It was like men handling a fish which is still alive and may jump back into the water. But he stood quite unresisting, yielding his arms limply to the ropes, as though he hardly noticed what was happening.

Eight o'clock struck and a bugle call, desolately thin in the wet air, floated from the distant barracks. The superintendent of the jail, who was standing apart from the rest of us, moodily prodding the gravel with his stick, raised his head at the sound. He was an army doctor, with a grey toothbrush moustache and a gruff voice. 'For God's sake hurry up, Francis,' he said irritably. 'The man ought to have been dead by this time. Aren't you ready yet?'

Francis, the head jailer, a fat Dravidian in a white drill suit and gold spectacles, waved his black hand. 'Yes sir, yes sir,' he bubbled. 'All is satisfactorily prepared. The hangman is waiting. We shall proceed.'

"Well, quick march, then. The prisoners can't get their breakfast till this job's over."

We set out for the gallows. Two warders marched on either side of the prisoner, with their rifles at the slope; two others marched close against him, gripping him by arm and shoulder, as though at once pushing and supporting him. The rest of us, magistrates and the like, followed behind. Suddenly, when we had gone ten yards, the procession stopped short without any order or warning. A dreadful thing had happened - a dog, come goodness knows whence, had appeared in the yard. It came bounding among us with a loud volley of barks, and leapt round us wagging its whole body, wild with glee at finding so many human beings together. It was a large woolly dog, half Airedale, half pariah. For a moment it pranced round us, and then, before anyone could stop it, it had made a dash for the prisoner, and jumping up tried to lick his face. Everyone stood aghast, too taken aback even to grab at the dog.

"Who let that bloody brute in here?" said the superintendent angrily. "Catch it, someone!"

A warder, detached from the escort, charged clumsily after the dog, but it danced and gambolled just out of his reach, taking everything as part of the game. A young Eurasian jailer picked up a handful of gravel and tried to stone the dog away, but it dodged the stones and came after us again. Its yaps echoed from the jail wails. The prisoner, in the grasp of the two warders, looked on incuriously, as though this was another formality of the hanging. It was several minutes before someone managed to catch the dog. Then we put my handkerchief through its collar and moved off once more, with the dog still straining and whimpering.

It was about forty yards to the gallows. I watched the bare brown back of the prisoner marching in front of me. He walked clumsily with his bound arms, but quite steadily, with that bobbing gait of the Indian who never straightens his knees. At each step his muscles slid neatly into place, the lock of hair on his scalp danced up and down, his feet printed themselves on the wet gravel. And once, in spite of the men who gripped him by each shoulder, he stepped slightly aside to avoid a puddle on the path.

It is curious, but till that moment I had never realized what it means to destroy a healthy, conscious man. When I saw the prisoner step aside to avoid the puddle, I saw the mystery, the unspeakable wrongness, of cutting a life short when it is in full tide. This man was not dying, he was alive just as we were alive. All the organs of his body were working - bowels digesting food, skin renewing itself, nails growing, tissues forming - all toiling away in solemn foolery. His nails would still be growing when he stood on the drop, when he was falling through the air with a tenth of a second to live. His eyes saw the yellow gravel and the grey walls, and his brain still remembered, foresaw, reasoned - reasoned even about puddles. He and we were a party of men walking together, seeing, hearing, feeling, understanding the same world; and in two minutes, with a sudden snap, one of us would be gone-one mind less, one world less.

The gallows stood in a small yard, separate from the main grounds of the prison, and overgrown with tall prickly weeds. It was a brick erection like three sides of a shed, with planking on top, and above that two beams and a crossbar with the rope dangling. The hangman, a grey-haired convict in the white uniform of the prison, was waiting beside his machine. He greeted us with a servile crouch as we entered. At a word from Francis the two warders, gripping the prisoner more closely than ever, half led, half pushed him to the gallows and helped him clumsily up the ladder. Then the hangman climbed up and fixed the rope round the prisoner's neck.

We stood waiting, five yards away. The warders had formed in a rough circle round the gallows. And then, when the noose was fixed, the prisoner began crying out on his god. It was a high, reiterated cry of 'Ram! Ram! Ram! Ram!', not urgent and fearful like a prayer or a cry for help, but steady, rhythmical, almost like the tolling of a bell. The dog answered the sound with a whine. The hangman, still standing on the gallows, produced a small cotton bag like a flour bag and drew it down over the prisoner's face. But the sound, muffled by the cloth, still persisted, over and over again: "Ram! Ram! Ram! Ram! Ram!"

The hangman climbed down and stood ready, holding the lever. Minutes seemed to pass. The steady, muffled crying from the prisoner went on and on, 'Ram! Ram! Ram!' never faltering for an instant. The superintendent, his head on his chest, was slowly poking the ground with his stick; perhaps he was counting the cries, allowing the prisoner a fixed number-fifty, perhaps, or a hundred. Everyone had changed colour. The Indians had gone grey like bad coffee, and one or two of the bayonets were wavering. We looked at the lashed, hooded man on the drop, and listened to his cries - each cry another second of life; the same thought was in all our minds: oh, kill him quickly, get it over, stop that abominable noise!

Suddenly the superintendent made up his mind. Throwing up his head he made a swift motion with his stick. 'Chalo!' he shouted almost fiercely.

There was a clanking noise, and then dead silence. The prisoner had vanished, and the rope was twisting on itself. I let go of the dog, and it galloped immediately to the back of the gallows; but when it got there it stopped short, barked, and then retreated into a corner of the yard, where it stood among the weeds, looking timorously out at us. We went round the gallows to inspect the prisoner's body. He was dangling with his toes pointed straight downwards, very slowly revolving, as dead as a stone.

The superintendent reached out with his stick and poked the bare body; it oscillated, slightly. 'He's all right,' said the superintendent. He backed out from under the gallows, and blew out a deep breath. The moody look had gone out of his face quite suddenly. He glanced at his wrist-watch. "Eight minutes past eight. Well, that's all for this morning, thank God."

The warders unfixed bayonets and marched away. The dog, sobered and conscious of having misbehaved itself, slipped after them. We walked out of the gallows yard, past the condemned cells with their waiting prisoners, into the big central yard of the prison. The convicts, under the command of warders armed with lathis, were already receiving their breakfast. They squatted in long rows, each man holding a tin pannikin, while two warders with buckets marched round ladling out rice; it seemed quite a homely, jolly scene, after the hanging. An enormous relief had come upon us now that the job was done. One felt an impulse to sing, to break into a run, to snigger. All at once everyone began chattering gaily.

The Eurasian boy walking beside me nodded towards the way we had come, with a knowing smile: "Do you know, sir, our friend (he meant the dead man), when he heard his appeal had been dismissed, he pissed on the floor of his cell. From fright. - Kindly take one of my cigarettes, sir. Do you not admire my new silver case, sir? From the boxwallah, two rupees eight annas. Classy European style."

Several people laughed-at what, nobody seemed certain.

Francis was walking by the superintendent, talking garrulously. 'Well, sir, all hass passed off with the utmost satisfactoriness. It was all finished-flick! Like that. It is not always so-oah, no! I have known cases where the doctor was obliged to go beneath the gallows and pull the prisoner's legs to ensure decease. Most disagreeable!'

"Wriggling about, eh? That's bad," said the superintendent.

"Ach, sir, it is worse when they become refractory! One man, I recall, clung to the bars of his cage when we went to take him out. You will scarcely credit, sir, that it took six warders to dislodge him, three pulling at each leg. We reasoned with him. "My dear fellow," we said, "think of all the pain and trouble you are causing to us!" But no, he would not listen! Ach, he was very troublesome!"

I found that I was laughing quite loudly. Everyone was laughing. Even the superintendent grinned in a tolerant way. "You'd better all come out and have a drink,' he said quite genially. 'I've got a bottle of whisky in the car. We could do with it."

We went through the big double gates of the prison, into the road. "Pulling at his legs!" exclaimed a Burmese magistrate suddenly, and burst into a loud chuckling. We all began laughing again. At that moment Francis's anecdote seemed extraordinarily funny. We all had a drink together, native and European alike, quite amicably. The dead man was a hundred yards away.

August, 1931

Response and Writing Assignments:

1.) Examine George Orwell's observations throughout the story. Are they highly detailed? Does his use of details add to his credibility and authority as a storyteller? Does he establish a sense of authority? Explain.

2.) What do you think the point of this essay is? Is Orwell for or against capital punishment? Cite examples from the text.

3.) Using his head and his heart, Orwell makes some very moving observations of the condemned man on the way to his execution. Cite them. How do these observations and images serve to support his thesis?

4.) What are Orwell's observations after the execution? What do these observations tell him about the others and himself?

5.) Which observations are more powerful in driving home Orwell's thesis, the execution or its aftermath? Explain.

Chapter Four: A Workable Thesis

To have something to say is a question of sleepless nights and worry and endless ratiocination of a subject-of endless trying to dig out of the essential truth, the essential justice.

— F. Scott Fitzgerald

The thesis is your main point, the heart and soul of your essay. It's your reason for writing, the center from which your entire composition will flow. Without a thesis, you don't have an essay, just a lot of rambling words, a hodgepodge of ideas with no particular purpose.

Each composition must be true to its thesis—all the way to its conclusion. You must support your thesis with topic sentences in each of the paragraphs which have to be carefully organized and flow from one to the next.

A thesis, especially in a freshman composition course, should be clearly stated. Don't merely imply your thesis, though some more artful, professional writers can get away with it. Your thesis should be to the point, one sentence long and self-contained, which means it should be able to stand alone. That means that if you were to circle it, or cut it out and paste it on a wall, everyone who read it would get your point. Examine the following:

"Though some analysts hold dim views of solar energy's market viability, soaring oil and gas prices, plus the possibility of alternative fuel tax credits, could soon give the solar industry its day in the sun."

There is no question here as to what your essay will be about. And speaking of questions, never posit your thesis as a question such as the following.

"Will high oil and gas prices help solar energy make a comeback?"

How should we know? You're the one writing the essay. Remember, these are thesis statements, not thesis questions.

Where do these come from? Everywhere! They can spring from the practical things we encounter in our daily lives to the meaning of life ones presented by George Orwell and Virginia Woolf. We recommend you steer clear of such broad "meaning of life" theses in your assignments. Again, leave such ethereal musings to established writers. Broad theses are unwieldy for novice writers to adequately handle in four-to 10-page class assignments.

For starters, seek out a simple, workable thesis. Ideas for them are everywhere, and opinions are in no short supply these days. Just check out blogs, bulletin boards, customer reviews on Amazon.com, etc. Peruse the "Letters to the Editor" in your local newspaper, which, according to Rule #1 (You can't be a good writer unless you're a good reader.), you should be reading regularly.

Begin by looking for a workable thesis, an opinion you have about something in your own world that has broader significance. I always suggest that students start by reading comments posted on the Web or reading a paper's letters section. These letters obviously have a point, a thesis, or else the editor would not waste precious space publishing them.

More importantly, most Letters to the Editor are to the point. They don't have the luxury of lengthy introductions. In fact, many of the short ones are theses in themselves. They deal with things that concern readers, issues that are either positive or negative, such as: taxes; the school budget; the federal deficit; the war in Iraq; poverty in America; rising fuel prices; rising crime; affordable housing; capital punishment; civil liberties; the separation of church and state. The topics can be as local as the need for a traffic light at a dangerous intersection or as global as the need to stop nuclear proliferation.

Letters to the Editor are also a good training ground when it comes to reading—and writing—much longer opinion pieces and argumentation essays. That's because the writers of these letters often do what all good writers of nonfiction must. That is, to focus locally while thinking globally. As a writer, letters also give you a chance to start out small. That is, you don't need to tackle a lengthy, multi-page essay to drive home your point. You can make it short, honing your thesis in the process.

By reading and writing such letters you will also remain true to the **Rule # 6, which calls for clarity and conciseness**. Also, having your letter published in your local paper or on the Web can be a terrific morale booster for the fledgling writer, as well as tangible proof of the power of the written word. It is always a thrill to see students ecstatically waving a copy of a newspaper or computer printout containing their letter. They feel vindicated because they have been published.

I will never forget the comment I heard 12 years ago from a South American student named Oscar Ortiz, who was enrolled in the first class I ever taught at Norwalk Community College. (The school was called Norwalk Community-Technical College at the time.) Writing with his head and his heart, Oscar had just finished an opinion piece about illegal immigration. And he was determined to publish it. He did. It ran as a "Letter to the Editor" in the Stamford Advocate, a Pulitzer Prize-winning, Connecticut, daily newspaper. The letter, prominently placed under a Pat Oliphant editorial cartoon and titled "By Pointing Blame at Immigrants We Obfuscate Issues," was published Easter Sunday, April 7, 1996. It also ran simultaneously in Greenwich Time, another Southern Connecticut daily.

"People are coming up to me at the deli counter and asking, 'Oscar, is this you?' " he said, noting that prior to being published he was basically ignored at the upscale Greenwich supermarket.

"I used to feel that the world was there, and I was here, and that what I thought wouldn't matter," he added. "Now, I have a voice."

What he said resonated because it was true. The best way to appreciate the power and effectiveness of writing is simply to write to be read, whether it is in your classroom or for a much larger audience. Start by voicing your opinion about something you hold dear, or something that irks you. It doesn't have to be monumental, but it has to be important to you, an issue that touches your head and your heart.

The following is Oscar's letter as it appeared:

To the Editor:

Are immigrants to blame for all the problems the United States is facing?

Most native-born Americans believe legal immigration is a threat to everyone in the United States. For more than 100 years the United States has been known as a land of immigrants. People have come from all corners of the world to make American what it is today. The freedom and opportunity it provides makes America the perfect place for many people. Suddenly America is the land of immigrants, but only the land of those who are already here.

There are those who argue current immigration laws are too restrictive and believe the vast majority of people who come to the United States are eager to work and be independent. An Urban Institute report, based on 1990 Census Bureau data, point out that only 4.7 percent of immigrants receive cash-assisted welfare, which is outweighed by the taxes paid by immigrants in general.

Other urban institutions agree that immigrant populations often revitalize local economies. In Miami, the number of Cuban-owned businesses skyrocketed from 919 in 1967 to 28,000 in 1990, making

Miami's economy stronger than ever before. Let's not forget: Most legal immigrants are raised and educated with somebody else's penny before they come here to work and pay taxes for the next 30 to 40 years. Not a bad deal for America.

We're a nation of immigrants, but we're attacking the newcomers. "Let's raise a fence along the border with Mexico," some say. Are we ready to take the place of those who cross the border to work in our farms for very low wages every season? Forces to "protect" the southern border will double in the next few years. Yet our northern border, Canada, is wide open to those who look American to come in and out as they please.

If the attitude of Americans toward immigrants 100 years ago had been like today's, many of us would not be here. We should not just allow anyone to come to the United States. But we should not see immigrants as our enemy. Instead, we should support legal immigration and continue to make America even bigger than it is today. We should stop blaming immigrants for the country's problems and take a good look around to find out what is really wrong.

I am a 29-year-old Colombian who immigrated to this great country 10 years ago. I became an American citizen four years ago. I am raising a family, working full time and currently attending night school at Norwalk Community-Technical College.

Oscar D. Ortiz

Stamford

Response Questions:

1.) Considering that this letter was written more than 12 years ago–and that immigration today remains a hot-button issue–does Oscar's argument seem prophetic? Is it persuasive?

2.) What is the author's thesis, and how does he balance logic and emotion to make his point?

3.) How does the author establish credibility with the audience?

4.) What type of research did the writer use to back up his thesis? Does it make his argument stronger? Explain.

What follows are letters written in a Norwalk Community College ENG 101 Composition class during the Fall 2007 semester. The first one, written by Christine Imbrogno, was published by Greenwich Time on Wednesday, Dec. 12, 2007. Ms. Imbrogno's reaction was the same as

Oscar's 11 years earlier, one of excitement and the thrill of having one's opinion shared with a large audience.

To the Editor:

In the early 1980s, the father of a dear friend of mine lost his life due to speeding on the Merritt Parkway late one evening. He left his 2-year-old daughter and wife at the Cos Cob home to go visit some old high school friends in upstate Connecticut.

The speed limit on the parkway was 55 mph. But he wasn't going 55 – he was going 82 when he lost control of his car and died after hitting one of the many bridge abutments on the sides of the road. He died instantly and caused a pileup due to his speeding/accident.

There are thousands of accidents that occur every single year on this 37.6 mile stretch of highway that runs through southern Connecticut. Why is the number so high? Because Connecticut state troopers don't find it imperative to monitor the speeding that happens on it!

My friend isn't the first or last person to lose a family member to an accident on this popular parkway. The number of casualties and accidents could decrease if only state troopers would spend more time along the on-and off-ramps on the Merritt. Why don't they find it important to control how fast people are driving? Not only is speeding dangerous to begin with, but mix in narrow roads and no street lights, and what do you get? Potentially hazardous driving conditions!

If more state troopers were patrolling the Merritt, not only would the number of accidents and casualties go down, but the state of Connecticut would find itself with so much extra money from tickets that is needed for the important things like education!

Christine Imbrogno

Cos Cob

Next, are some letters penned in the same class, letters that didn't make it into print but were worthy of publication.

To the Editor:

I do so enjoy a good cup of coffee. On occasion I will order one of those foamy, sweet, whipped delights but usually I just have a decaffeinated with cream. Of course I would prefer to drink regular coffee. Regular is generally fresher, there are often a number of flavor choices and everyone knows, it just tastes better. Unfortunately for me, palpitations, nausea and trembling are not worth the indulgence. So I take my fix however I can get it.

When getting a hot drink at one of the many coffee places in this area, I will ask for, "A small decaf with cream, please." It sounds straightforward enough but at least two times out of every ten I receive regular coffee. Sadly, I only realize this after consuming the whole cup and finding myself in the midst of my caffeine induced misery. Is it really that hard to get my simple order correct? Is it because they ran out of decaf? I would happily wait a few minutes for a new pot to be brewed. Did the server not hear me clearly? Do they just not like decaf drinkers? I try to minimize my chances of getting fueled coffee. I no longer use the drive through. I stand at the counter and obnoxiously stare at the preparation of my beverage. I have even taken on the annoying trait of questioning, sometimes more than once, "Is this definitely decaf?" I am always given assurances that it is.

A couple of weeks ago, I stopped at my local coffee shop. I was helping a friend to pack for a move and a hot beverage was just what I needed. As usual, I ordered a decaf for myself and a regular for my friend, paid the server and left a generous tip. I politely asked, "Which one is decaf?" The server wordlessly pointed at a 'D' marked on one of the lids. I took my cups and had drunk half of mine before arriving at my friend's house. About 30 minutes or so later, I discovered that I could no longer wrap dishes in newspaper as my hands were shaking so badly. I was not allowed near the breakables after that although I did single-handedly pack up two cars with numerous heavy boxes!

Later that night in bed, I was exhausted yet unable to relax. I tossed and turned but was incapable of focusing even on a simple task like reading. As my mind abstractly churned, it came to me that the 'D' on my cup was not for 'decaf' after all but actually stood for 'deceived' as it seemed I had been yet again.

Yours in frustration,
Emma Villavicencio

To the Editor:

I go shopping a few times a week at Costco Warehouse on Rt. 1 in Norwalk. The moment I turn into the Costco parking lot, I find myself in a parking nightmare. There are at least two cars in line waiting for each parking space close to the store entrance to free up. These waiting cars block both cars and people trying to move around the parking lot and to enter the garage. I do not understand why shoppers insist on parking above ground next to the store entrance when there are plenty of parking spaces in the garage. The garage has an elevator and it is very easy to enter and exit the store.

It seems to me that many people are interested in reducing the amount of walking that they have to do. They would rather spend their time sitting in their car, waiting for a parking space to open up, than simply park in the first space they find and walk to the store. It is no surprise that obesity has become so prevalent here in the past few years. The solution is not the quick solutions advertised on TV, for example weight loss pills. "Alli", one of the most recent in a long string of quick fix diet pills has recently been linked with the need to have bypass surgery. The solution for obesity is exercising and a healthy diet. A short walk to and from the store entrance will do more for a person's health and will reduce the aggravation of all shoppers trying to move around the parking lot.

I am also dismayed by the attitude of people who park and shop at Costco. There seems to be an attitude of personal entitlement and a total lack of acknowledgement of other people. Shoppers who have finished their shopping and are loading up their car do not seem to care that there is someone waiting for their parking space and that a traffic jam is developing. The shoppers seem to just take their time, only thinking about themselves. Shoppers waiting in their cars lose their tempers, honk their horns and curse at other shoppers.

I wonder if all the advantages that we have here in the U.S. in some way contributes to the rudeness and selfishness that we see? In Europe, you would walk and think nothing of it. If you wanted a grocery bag, you would pay for it. If you wanted the use of a shopping cart, you would make a deposit and (here is the best part), you would only get that deposit back when you returned the shopping cart back to its stall.

In looking for a solution, I wonder if Costco would consider, especially during this busy shopping season, to have an employee working as a traffic director in the parking lot to help the shoppers move in and out more smoothly. Perhaps this together with a little more awareness on our part of our own behavior would make for a healthier and more pleasant shopping experience.

Violet Karacsony

To the Editor:

I would like to share what happened to me some time ago, when I was coming home from downtown Stamford.

It was evening and I was driving back from one of Stamford's shopping centers. As I approached the intersection of Summer Street and Bank Street, the light changed red. I stopped on the left line. On my right there was a police car waiting to turn right. With the green light I turned left, but I also noticed that the cop, instead of turning right, decided to follow me. After crossing a few intersections the cop pulled me over. I thought that my vehicle and driving were impeccable. When the cop walked up to my car he asked me to step out of the vehicle. He cuffed me and put me in a police car without any explanation. When I asked him what it was all about, he basically told me to shut up. In the meantime, at least six more police cars arrived. They were blocking the street like there was some big crime going on.

After a short conversation with his colleagues, the cop that stopped me finally asked for my driver's license. I asked again why I was being treated like that. He told me that the license plate on my car belonged to a different vehicle. I told him that it was impossible and that the registration card was in the glove compartment. A few minutes later the officer came back with my documents. He let me out of his car and explained that there was a mistake in the system. His sources showed him that the plate belonged on my old car that I got rid of a couple of months ago.

Back then, I transferred the plates onto my newer vehicle. Unfortunately, the Department of Motor Vehicles did not make the changes in the system that caused my unpleasant experience with the cops. The law enforcement, however, could have taken different steps in investigating this error. I do not understand why I was not asked for my license and registration at first. Both vehicles were registered in my name, and the officer could have figure out earlier that it was a mistake. He did not have to treat me like a criminal. On the other hand, DMV officers responsible for entering information into the system should be more painstaking and scrupulous. My case was not only a rare coincidence. I know of more similar events that were caused by exactly the same DMV error. Therefore, I would like to address my case to DMV workers to make sure that they complete their tasks, as well as to police officers who, in my opinion, sometimes overdo their job.

Marcin Cwalina

Response Questions:

1.) Which of the above letters did you find the most interesting? The most amusing? The most disconcerting?

2.) How did each of the writers establish a sense of authority in each of the letters? Which letter had the most passion? Did it do so at the expense of logic?

Assignments:

1.) Read the "Letters to the Editor" section of your local newspaper over several days. What are the key issues that concern readers? List them.

2.) What is the average length of the letters that appear? Does each of these letters have a clearly defined thesis? If not, which ones do? Write them down.

3.) What issues in the "Letters" section interest you most? Is there a hot-button issue that concerns you that is not being addressed by the letters? Would you like to write one?

4.) Attempt to write such a letter. Begin by writing your main point, your thesis, in a clear, declarative sentence. Is your thesis clear? Is it self-contained? Is it a statement or a question?

5.) In your letter, support your thesis with at least three major points that you will present in at least three small paragraphs. Most newspaper paragraphs are short, usually no more than a few sentences.

6.) When writing your letter, make sure your paragraphs flow from one idea to the other. The flow is aided by what we call transitions. Transitions are made by key words, phrases, and a logical presentation of facts. There are sequential transitions, such as: first, second, third, next and furthermore. Sometimes, transitions are made by juxtapositions, such as these phrases: on the contrary, on the other hand, conversely, however. Some transitions are helped by words that lead to a logical deduction, such as the word therefore. We will be discussing transitions at length in a later chapter. The point is for you to make sure that your letter, as short as it is, flows logically from one paragraph to the other to help support your thesis.

7.) Polish your letter and read it in class. What kind of reaction did it get? Are you ready to send it out for publication? Most editors today prefer to receive their letters via email because it saves them the time of having to key in copy. What is the email address of the editor who handles this section? What are some of the requirements and restrictions that they put on letters?

8.) Is there are book you have read or would like to read? Go to Amazon.com and find the book. If you have read the book, you obviously have an opinion on it. Was it terrible or was it terrific? How did it meet your expectations, or how did it disappoint? Amazon.com actively seeks out reader input and reviews, again, with your name attached. What is your view? Again, make sure your thesis is clear.

9.) You can state your opinion, your thesis, via comments to various web logs, or blogs. A number of online newspapers routinely look for reader comments to stories. These are golden opportunities, if you remain true to the Seven Rules of Good Writing, to hone the ability to craft powerful thesis statements.

10.) Make a list of at least 10 other topics or issues that interest or concern you. Which ones generate the most interest and emotion? What do you have to say about them that had not been already said? What about your perception is unique? Which ones would be subjects for your next letters?

Chapter Five: Beyond the Blog

They seem omnipresent in cyberspace—Web logs, what are commonly referred to as blogs. *MySpace.com*, for example, has entries for myriad categories, from politics and religion to the concerns of pet owners to celebrity scandals to relationships, automotive tips, etc.

In other words, as we saw in the previous chapter, there is no short supply of opinions on every topic. People have them, and they want to share them, whether it takes the form of blogging, writing Letters to the Editor, or literally just getting up on the proverbial soapbox, though the latter is about as rare these days as soapboxes are.

Much of what you find on sites like *MySpace.com* and *Xanga,* as examples, is a wonderful portal into how people feel about the world around them. Readers get to know what others are thinking, to take the world's intellectual and emotional pulse, if you will.

And that's what true democracy is, citizen participation, your voice being heard. To that end, blogs are a communications breakthrough, as invaluable to the computer age as the Penny Press was to Colonial America.

That's not to say that all blogs, or Letters to the Editor for that matter, are masterfully done. While some evoke the right balance between logic and emotion, not to mention ethics and credibility, most seem like not-so-well-thought-out mouthing off, cyber venting, or as stated earlier, a keyboard catharsis.

It's not that the opinions expressed are not valid. It's that oftentimes blogs don't do valid opinions the justice they deserve. Emotion, the pathos, seems to dominate. Logic, the logos, seems to take a back seat. Why? Because the opinions are not carefully planned and presented. Sensationalism seems to dominate. It almost seems as if the writers feel that getting noticed is the primary end, the quality of the argument the secondary one.

Examine the following blogs entered on MySpace.com over Memorial Day weekend. The first was submitted by an individual named Michael on Monday, May 29, 2006.

Memorial Day for the Nothings

Today of course is Memorial Day: The day of remembrance for all the soldiers who have died fighting for our freedom. When we think of Memorial Day (if we think of it at all beyond BBQ's and an extra day off work) we usually always think of heroics. We think of the World War II veterans who died fighting on the beaches of Normandy, or in some huge gunfight pushing back the Nazi army in Africa.

But I think we should take a moment and remember the soldiers that died for well.. nothing. Let's remember the soldiers who gave their life in battles that had little to do with anything beyond our leaders in a pissing contest with our enemy du jour. Let's not forget all the soldiers that died in Iraq and Afghanistan stopping a threat that didn't exist. Let's not forget all the soldiers that died in secret operations trying to keep warlords and dictators from closing our trade lanes in far away places. Because when Memorial Day rolls around we all tend to forget that a number of soldiers and good Americans die simply for the whims and failure of our leaders to accept responsibility for their actions, or admit mistakes. They aren't celebrated, or honored. There will be no statues made for them, and no country singers will write songs for them, but in the end these soldiers that die simply because of our leaders failures are just as heroic and deserve all of our respect. - until next time.

Response Questions:

1.) Examine the blog closely. What is Michael's thesis?

2.) It is obvious from the first line of the second paragraph that Michael believes most soldiers have died in vain, the unwilling dupes of individuals in power who were looking to protect their own interests. Do you agree or disagree? How much of your opinion comes from what Michael writes or from other sources?

3.) Does Michael prove his point, or is he just spewing? Does he balance his emotion with logic by using credible examples?

4.) Does Michael back up his opinions with credible sources? Does he succeed or fail in establishing authority on the subject?

5.) Do you see this blog as the beginning of a powerful, thought provoking essay? If so, what will it need to succeed? How can it be better developed?

6.) Finally, what about the writing itself. How effective is it? How is it hampered by the need for editing? Please edit Michael's blog for grammar, spelling, and punctuation.

Examine the following blog, "Gadgets, Gadgets Everywhere," entered by an individual named Dawn on May 30, 2006.

Okay people, I am now part of the 21st century.

Heh. My close friends know that I will never buy myself fun, cool stuff unless it is for strictly practical and utilitarian purposes. I love gadgets, but I won't buy it unless I need it. This is good, because if I do buy it, I'm gonna put down some serious cash and make sure it is good. Like my home computer. I upgraded the heck out of it, so I would be happy with it for at least 3 years.

The only time I have gone against this good judgment is the LCD wide screen TV I bought a few months ago. A 27" CRT really is too big for me to move easily, so I wanted to get a flat panel, so I can pick it up (I redecorate and rearrange often). The problem is that I don't have $2K to blow on a TV. So I bought an off-brand one for $700. And I am paying for it. I already need to take it in to get repaired.

So why am I now part of the 21st century in gadgetry? I, my dear readers, am now a proud owner of my very first iPod!

My wonderful, awesome boyfriend, Mark, surprised me with an iPod nano on Friday, complete with five different color jelly sleeves to suit my every mood. He even ripped all the CD's I had left in his car from our last trip, and added them to my new player.

We took it on our getaway this weekend (blog on the trip forthcoming as soon as I get all the pics ready). We had brought speakers, but we ended up going to Wal-Mart to find something portable so we could take it on a picnic. Mark ended up buying me a very nice portable speaker/iPod docking station. He also picked up some socks for my iPod. I love that man. Of course, Mark has a slight ulterior motive in that he is trying to get me to see the almighty computer glory that is a Mac. The iPod is just the first step. We shall see.

Response Questions:

1.) What does the iPod represent to Dawn?
2.) Does she hold your interest? Does she build a connection with the reader?
3.) What type of audience is she writing for?
4.) What is the main point, the thesis, of Dawn's blog?
5.) Does she establish a sense of authority? How?
6.) This is the type of blog that may best be termed an Online Diary. Do you see it as such? How?

7.) What does Dawn learn about herself as a result of getting an iPod?

8.) Edit Dawn's blog for grammar, spelling and punctuation?

That last exercise may seem moot to many students. They will claim that Standard English grammar does not apply to blogs the same way we needn't be sticklers about grammar and punctuation with emails and IMs. Perhaps that is true for the blogging medium — but only if the blog or the email is seen as a draft, not a final product.

Proper grammar and Standard English usage is essential to making your writing the best it can be.

I bring this up now to show you that many blogs, despite what blogging fans might hold, are works in progress. They are the beginnings of what can be powerful essays, compositions that will inform, educate, entertain, and enrich readers' lives. They are quick bites for an opinion-hungry, information ravenous culture. I won't go as far as calling them informational junk food, but even blogging aficionados will agree, most blogs are far from nutritious, well-balanced, satisfying meals.

So the challenge begins: How do we go beyond the blog? How do we take an idea told succinctly in a couple or few paragraphs and flesh it out into a powerful essay? Again, by balancing logic and emotion. As you peruse blogging sites you will see that many entries are rich in emotion but lacking in logic. It's not that these entries are illogical, but that the opinions presented do not have enough research or credible evidence to support them.

Look at the "Memorial Day for Nothings" blog again. Michael makes some grabbing, controversial points sure to stoke passions, even outrage, among those who serve and their families. He also leaves the reader thinking, something that is the hallmark of a good essay. But how much logos is present? Does he prove his argument? Not really. The blog seems to show that the writer relied upon opinion and heated emotions to carry the piece, no questions asked. Such Pieces, unfortunately, run the risk of being all sizzle and no steak. After a while, listeners lose interest.

Of the many reasons why you can't rely upon emotion alone is that, simply put, it insults your reader's intelligence. Readers are much savvier that, perhaps due to years of emotional bombardment from the advertising, entertainment, and media industries. Don't get me wrong.

Emotion is a very powerful communications tool, but alone it can't carry the day.

Among the written word's greatest offenders when it comes to emotion trumping logic are tabloid newspapers, and not just the supermarket kind. Often they promise a sensational read via a grabber headline only to disappoint the reader with a short, not-so-meaty story on the inside. The reason there is more sizzle that steak is that the story has a lot of fat, necessary for taste, but lean on meat, such as the facts, figures, authoritative quotes, and ultimately, credibility. Since there is little *logos* to support the *pathos*, we are lest with a dearth of *ethos*.

Now that we made a case for and against the importance of blogs in expressing opinions, let's examine an essay with a thesis similar to Michael's about Memorial Day. The following is "Monday is Memorial Day! An Essay" posted on the DemocraticUnderground.com on Friday, May 26, 2006 at 10:50 a.m. Note that the essay was posted as a blog. It has no author, except to note that it was edited by someone with the screen name *rateyes*.

Still, the title makes it very clear that it is an essay.

Monday is Memorial Day. It's the holiday each year, celebrated on the last Monday in May, to remind us of those who gave their lives in service to our nation. It used to be called Decoration Day, because people would go (as some still do) to the graves of Americans who were killed in battle and decorate them with our country's flag as well as flowers and other items. Tomorrow, as is tradition, the person who occupies the Oval Office will go to Arlington Cemetery and place a wreath at the Tomb of the Unknowns . . . a memorial that is there to remind us of the terrible price of war and the enormous cost of securing the blessings of liberty.

Memorials are important. As the word implies, memorials are used to remind us of important people and/or events. Memorials come in all shapes, sizes and forms, and are everywhere we go. In fact, some memorials are so commonplace that we forget that they are, in fact, memorials. We see them-monuments or other symbols designed to evoke a memory-and, we don't remember, at least we don't remember to the extent that we should remember.

Some memorials, by the way, are being hidden from us in the hopes that we won't "remember." The flag-draped coffins coming home from Iraq and Afghanistan are memorials to the lies that we have been told by those who have broken their pledge to "protect and defend the Constitution from all enemies, foreign and domestic."

A memorial is erected, not only for those erecting it to help them remember—but, also to TEACH lessons to those who come later who were not there to see the event or to know the person for whom the memorial stands. That's why we should be allowed to see those flag-draped coffins. But, I digress.

I'll never forget as a child of about 10 years of age, standing inside the Lincoln Memorial in Washington D.C. looking into the stone face of the giant man sitting in that chair, and walking out from that building looking in the same direction Lincoln faces and seeing that grand spire that almost touches the sky, named after the first U.S. President and seeing the flags of the various states which encircle that monument . . . and, then seeing to the right across the water a circular building honoring the man who authored the Virginia Statue for Religious Liberty, which became the basis for the Constitution's first amendment's protection guaranteeing the separation of church and state, as well as the Declaration of Independence.

I had heard about those men in school. I didn't know much about them . . . but, seeing those memorials made me want to learn more about them. And as I did learn more about them, and had the opportunity to go back a second time years later, seeing those memorials again filled me with a sense of awe and wonder at the sacrifices that those men, and other men and women who are memorialized on that mall, made to secure and protect the blessings of liberty that many of us take for granted.

None of us here today were alive during the times of Washington and Jefferson, and Lincoln. But, yet, when we see those memorials we REMEMBER them, don't we? Or rather, we REMEMBER THE LESSONS they and their contemporaries, both men and women, taught us as those lessons were passed on to us from generation to generation—memories kept alive, in part, by the memorials that stand in their honor.

Each and every year, thousands upon thousands of school children walk that mall in Washington D.C. on class field-trips. They see the monuments to great people, to bloody battles, to human achievement, and to unknown heroes. They are taken there to impress upon them the lessons of history. That's the main reason for memorials. . . to TEACH THE CHILDREN the history of their people.

And, since that is the case: I want to ask a simple question of you today. "What memorials are we establishing for our children, today?" What is it that we are leaving behind in our wake that will speak of who we are, what we did, and what trials we overcame? And, when our children and grandchildren and great-grandchildren ask their parents what they mean, will the remembrances be good or bad? Will the lessons taught be honorable ones? For, you see, we erect memorials to both the good and the bad. Yes, we have a Washington Monument. But, we also have a U.S.S. Arizona Memorial at Pearl Harbor. Yes, we have Mt. Rushmore. But, we also have empty chairs in another park where the Murrah Federal Building once stood in Oklahoma City. And, today the statue that we call "Lady Liberty" looks across the waters to a memorial being built at Ground Zero.

Will the memorials we build as one generation of Americans speak of love or hate, war or peace, justice or injustice, inclusion or exclusion, division or unity, building up the nation or tearing it apart?

Make no mistake, our history is being written, carved in stone and left behind for all the future generations to read . . . and someday, a long time from now, someone will read that history and make judgments about whether or not we lived up to our self-proclaimed title as the "greatest nation on earth." Our grandchildren will judge us by our history we write and the legacy they inherit from us. From the memorials we leave behind for them, what lessons will they learn?

Response Questions:

1.) Do you agree with the author that this is an essay, or is it more of a blog?

2.) How does *rateyes'* writing compare to Michael's blog? Does it seem more or less authoritative? Why?

3.) Does this author establish credibility? Explain.

4.) What is this author's thesis? Is it stated directly or implied?

5.) What do you think of the author's use of facts to support the thesis?

6.) Is the author's thesis reiterated in the conclusion?

7.) Does the conclusion leave you thinking? Explain.

The next example is an Opinion-Editorial that appeared in WSJ.com, The Opinion Journal of the Wall Street Journal. Written by Christopher Hitchens, an author and national columnist, this piece appeared in an extremely respected publication, as the Wall Street Journal is the most revered financial publication in the world.

REFLECTIONS ON
THOSE WHO MADE THE ULTIMATE SACRIFICE
By Christopher Hitchens
Monday, May 29, 2006 12:01 a.m. EDT

LONDON—In the Cotswold hills, in deep England, there is a pair of villages named Upper Slaughter and Lower Slaughter. In addition to

its rather gruesome name, Lower Slaughter possesses a unique distinc-
tion. It is the only village in all of England that does not possess a First
World War memorial. In the remainder of the country, even the small-
est hamlet will have—I almost said "will boast"—a stone marker with
an arresting number of names on it. In bigger towns, it wouldn't be
possible to incise all the names in stone, though at the Menin Gate in
the Belgian town of Ypres a whole arch is inscribed with the names of
those who fell along the Somme. Every year on Nov. 11–anniversary of
the 1918 "Armistice"—the rest of the English-speaking world gathers,
with Flanders poppies worn in the lapel, to commemorate the dead of
all wars but in particular to feel again the still-aching wounds of the
"war to end all wars": the barbaric conflict that shook peoples' faith in
civilization itself.

Though the carnage of that war was felt much less in the United
States, it was only after the doughboys returned in 1918 that the for-
mer Confederate states dropped their boycott of America's original
"Memorial Day," proclaimed by Union commander Gen. John Logan
in May 1868. And here one can note the bizarre manner in which
war—which is division by definition—exerts its paradoxically uni-
fying effect. If it is "the health of the state," as was sardonically said
by that great foe of "Mr. Wilson's war," Randolph Bourne, then it can
also be an agent of emancipation and nation-building and even (as was
proved after 1945) of democracy. But even this reflection can never
abolish the insoluble problem: how to estimate the value of those whose
lives were cruelly cut off before victory was in sight. It is sometimes
rather lazily said that these soldiers "gave" their lives. It would be
equally apt, if more blunt, to say that they had their lives taken.
Humanity has been grappling with this conundrum ever since Pericles
gave his funeral oration, and there would have been many Spartan and
Melian widows and orphans who would have been heartily sickened
by those Athenian-centered remarks.

The soil of the United States is almost spoiled for choice when it comes
to commemorative sites. They range from Gettysburg itself—still one
of the most staggering places of memory in the world—to the
Confederate statue of Gen. Nathan Bedford Forrest, one of the founders
of the Ku Klux Klan, and extend from the Polar Bear monument in
Detroit (honoring those Michiganders who helped invade Russia in
1919: a forgotten war if ever there was one) to Maya Lin's masterpiece
of Vietnam understatement on the National Mall. But Memorial Day
transcends the specific, and collectivizes all disparate recollections into
one single reflection upon the losses inflicted by war itself. The summa

of this style, and one that transcends Pericles, is of course the Gettysburg Address, in which one cannot distinguish which side's graves are actually being honored. It was always Mr. Lincoln's way to insist that he was the elected president of every state, not just the "Northern" ones, and this speech still has the power to stir us because it was the most strenuous possible test of that essential proposition.

A memorial to, and for, all is certainly an improvement on the Arc de Triomphe/Brandenburg Gate style, which was regnant until 1918 and which asserted national exclusivity. Kemal Ataturk did a noble thing when he raised a monument to all those who fell at Gallipoli, and informed the British and Australian peoples that their "Tommies and Johnnies" would lie with his "Alis and Mehmets." But there are also disadvantages to a memorial that is too "inclusive." Not even President Reagan's fine speech at the cliffs of Pointe du Hoc has erased his crass equation of the "victims" at Bitburg cemetery with their victims. Bitburg is not Gettysburg: Some wounds cannot and perhaps should not be healed. The opposite danger also exists: Our "Memorial Day" is now the occasion of a three-day holiday weekend (over the protest of the Veterans of Foreign Wars) and has become somewhat banal precisely because it seems to honor nobody in particular.

The stark concept of "The Unknown Soldier" was the best expression of awe and respect that the century of total war managed to produce. Rudyard Kipling, whose only son, John, was posted as "missing" in 1915 (and whose remains were not found until 15 years ago) was the designer of the official headstone for those soldiers who lay in mass graves and could not even be identified. No pacifist, he nonetheless wrote with scorn of the "jelly-bellied flag-flappers" who lectured schoolboys on the glories of combat. Over time, it is the bleak poetry of Wilfred Owen, and not the inspirational verse of Julian Grenfell and Rupert Brooke, that has come to express the more profound experiences of warfare. Some thoughts must always lie too deep for tears.

Since all efforts at commemoration are bound to fall short, one must be on guard against any attempt at overstatement. In particular, one must resist efforts to ventriloquize the dead. To me, Cindy Sheehan's posthumous conscription of her son is as objectionable as Billy Graham's claim, at the National Cathedral, that all the dead of Sept. 11, 2001 were now in paradise. In the first instance, we have no reason to believe that young Casey Sheehan would ever have supported MoveOn.org, and in the second instance we cannot be expected to believe that almost 3,000 New Yorkers all died in a state of grace. Nothing is more tasteless, when set against the reality of death, than the hollow note of demagogy and

false sentiment. These things are also subject to unintended conse-
quences. When Dalton Trumbo wrote his leftist antiwar classic "Johnnie
Got His Gun," he little expected that it would be used as a propaganda
tool by pro-fascist isolationists in the late 1930s, and that he would be
protesting in vain that this was not what he had really meant.

"Always think of it: never speak of it." That was the stoic French injunc-
tion during the time when the provinces of Alsace and Lorraine had
been lost. This resolution might serve us well at the present time, when
we are in midconflict with a hideous foe, and when it is too soon to be
thinking of memorials to a war not yet won. This Memorial Day, one
might think particularly of those of our fallen who also guarded polling-
places, opened schools and clinics, and excavated mass graves. They rep-
resent the highest form of the citizen, and every man and woman among
them was a volunteer. This plain statement requires no further rhetoric.

Christopher Hitchens, a columnist for Vanity Fair, is the author of
"Thomas Jefferson: Author of America" (HarperCollins, 2005).

Response Questions:

1.) What is Hitchens' thesis? Is it clearly stated or implied?

2.) Is the essay easy to follow? For what type of audience is Hitchens writing?

3.) What kinds of words does Hitchens use to drive home the horrors of war?

4.) Does this essay seem well organized, or does it seem disjointed?

5.) Does Hitchens establish authority? Why or why not?

6.) Do you feel that Hitchens shows empathy for service people, and that he conveys that empathy well to his readers?

7.) Of the three pieces you have read on Memorial Day, how would you rate Hitchens' essay, first, second, or third? Explain.

8.) Disregarding that this essay was published in the highly respected Wall Street Journal, how would you grade it: High Pass, Pass, Low Pass, or Not Passing? Explain your answer.

9.) How would you improve the essay?

Chapter Six: Finding the Human Component

How does one best convey the human element of a story? By developing empathy for the individuals being written about and conveying that dimension, that human denominator that we all share, to the audience. You touch others best when you use words to show what touches you. What stirs and moves us is an intricate mix of what we observe, our perceptions of the world, our unique memories, and our commonality with all of humanity.

Examine the following, somewhat abbreviated story about a homeless woman, "When a Car is a Home in Westport," that I wrote for the Connecticut section of the New York Times back on Oct. 24, 1993.

Ans Jepkes smiled, twirled her long brown hair and reminisced about her life in Westport since she came from the Netherlands with her husband 20 years ago. She and her husband owned a three-bedroom Colonial off South Compo Road, a fashionable row of large houses with manicured lawns framed by stone walls. Her two boys learned to swim and sail at the local club. She took an active interest in their schools. And as her husband's international courier business prospered, Mrs. Jepkes said, she moved in the right social circles.

She stopped twirling her hair to adjust her blue jacket against the autumn chill. Last nightwas a cold one, she said, and tonight looked like more of the same. Heavy blankets would be in order. These days, Mrs. Jepkes, 40, is divorced, lives alone and sleeps in her car.

Sometimes she is awakened by tapping on the car window and the white glare from a police officer's flashlight. Then she drives around town in her 1986 Ford Mustang convertible and looks for another parking space to finish the night. In the back seat is a nest of blankets, a package of soda crackers and a teddy bear that belonged to her infant daughter whose custody she recently lost.

Mrs. Jepkes said she was concerned that she had not brushed her teeth on this day. She still wears fashionable clothes she bought herself, but she now prefers dark colors, she said, since stains do not show as much.

"I sit on a lot of curbs," said Mrs. Jepkes, as she waited for dinner at the Gillespie Center, the town-run soup kitchen and shelter for homeless men on Jesup Green. "When I see old friends, they act like they don't see me."

Mrs. Jepkes is one of several homeless women in an affluent suburb who manage to blend in with the downtown bustle. And as a result, their needs have gone largely unnoticed.

Westport has had homeless shelters for men for more than a decade, and Interfaith Housing Association of Westport-Weston, Inc., a local non-profit, social service agency, runs shelters for women with children in three town-owned houses. But no such shelter exists for single women.

For the past several years, Interfaith Housing has been campaigning to open a shelter for single women in Westport, but the effort has been resisted by town officials. First Selectman Douglas Wood argued, "When you're talking about municipalities that are not that large, they are not going to offer every kind of shelter." In addition to three homes and the men's shelter, he said, the town has a home for teen-age girls and a half-way house for homeless men recovering from alcoholism. "It doesn't make economic sense to set up another shelter when there are very few people who need it," Mr. Wood said.

Women account for about 20 percent of the estimated 15,300 homeless people who stayed in Connecticut shelters during the 1992 fiscal year, said a spokeswoman for the State Department of Social Services, Donna Jolly.

Since last spring, when the Westport Transit District moved its offices from the building housing the Gillespie Center, the Rev. Peter Powell, executive director of Interfaith Housing, has petitioned to use the space for a women's shelter. Elizabeth Cornell, a caseworker at the Gillespie Center, said that once the space was upgraded for code requirements and renovated with a shower, it could accommodate four women.

The homeless women are allowed to take free showers at the town's Y.M.C.A. But during the summer, Mrs. Jepkes said, she strolls by Longshore Beach Club, where she was once a member, and sneaks the use of the outdoor shower.

While a four-bed shelter is not a big one, Mrs. Cornell said, other women could at least sleep on the floor in emergencies. Meanwhile, she said, she has the painful task of sending away women who want to spend the night, no matter how cold. Town ordinances, she said, forbid homeless men and women from sleeping in the same quarters.

"But when the temperatures are life threatening, what can you do?" asked Charlotte Prince, a member of the board of Interfaith Housing. "We don't want to find anyone dead."

The closest single women's shelter is in Fairfield, but it only has five beds, and there is a long waiting list, Mrs. Cornell said. There are women's shelters in nearby South Norwalk and Bridgeport, but the Westport women are reluctant to stay there, "because they don't feel safe," said the Rev. Theodore Hoskins, pastor of the Saugatuck Congregational Church in Westport.

"They don't have the urban background, the skills to survive in that sort of setting," said Mr. Hoskins, adding that most of Westport's homeless women either grew up in town or have lived there for many years. "And that's what shelter is all about, safety and security."

Even though these women are homeless, most are not immune to Westport's social pressures. Mr. Hoskins said that one woman, for example, sometimes went without eating so she could save up for hair styling. "It's a vestige of pride that comes with a certain upbringing and a sense of your relationship," he said.

. . . Being destitute was the last things Mrs. Jepkes said she ever imagined. Her life began to fall apart, she said, following a divorce six years ago.

"I had two kids, and the money he was paying me wasn't enough. So I lived off my credit cards," she said. "I owed money to everybody."

In the meantime, she had met another man, became pregnant and wanted to keep the baby. She then put her home on the market to get out of debt, she said, and had her baby. After the mortgage, taxes and other costs were paid, Mrs. Jepkes walked away with $38,000, much of which went to pay off her credit cards and other bills, she said.

She and the man broke up, and Mrs. Jepkes lived with her infant daughter at a friend's house, in motels and later in her car. She said the baby now lived with her father. Her 18-year-old son now lives with her ex-husband in California, she said, and her 12-year-old son stays with Mrs. Jepkes' sister in Westport, which is the main reason she stays in town. She added that her sister had no room for her. Mrs. Jepkes sometimes drives to her son's school to see him, she said.

"The last time I saw him, I asked him for $10 for gas," she said. "He gave it to me. I think he feels funny."

A half-hour before lunch at the Gillespie Center, Mrs. Jepkes sat on a metal folding chair outside, smoked a cigarette and chatted with one of the homeless men. When she looked up, she saw Linda Fancher, a volunteer, dropping of trays of hot lunches that were donated by the Food Emporium.

"Hi, Ans," said Mrs. Fancher, whose daughter had been in the same class as Mrs. Jepkes' son.

Mrs. Jepkes politely smiled and resumed talking to the man.

"It's so embarrassing to have her see me like this," she said.

She took a deep drag, shrugged off the embarrassment and continued her conversation.

There were too many practical things to think about. The blankets. Money for gas. Another parking space.

Prior to this story's appearance, other publications' articles about homeless women in Westport, a highly affluent Connecticut suburb, did not focus on individuals. The women written about had been generalized. We never got to know them. They were abstractions, statistics. And, how much emotion can you feel for a statistic? I knew that a living, breathing individual would much better serve this story. Fortunately through contacts and sources I found Ans who agreed to be interviewed.

No sooner had Ans' story appeared that changes were afoot. I received a phone call at home from Joseph Arcudi, who was running for the town's first selectman.

"I want you to know that those women are going to get a shelter," Arcudi said in his signature, brusque cadence.

With the election two weeks away, I doubted it was just another campaign promise. It was too late to grandstand on the issue of homelessness. Joe Arcudi appeared to be speaking from the heart despite his gruff, often politically incorrect swagger. Following his election and inauguration in November, he kept his word.

As the new three-member Board of Selectman met for the first time, one of the first official acts was to approve the opening a shelter for homeless women.

That December as I trekked along Westport's downtown and trendy shops, a woman called out to me.

"Jim, come here," yelled Liz Cornell of the Gillespie Center. "I want to show you."

Through a narrow alley I followed her to the once empty rooms behind the soup kitchen. New carpeting had been put down. Several well-to-do Westport women, including the late actress Brett Somers, Jack Klugman's real-life wife who played his ex-wife on "The Odd Couple," were rearranging furniture and furnishings. The women's shelter was near completion.

"See what your article did!" exclaimed Mrs. Cornell.

I felt humbled and not as bad as I did before I walked in.

Ans wouldn't freeze to death before Christmas.

This moment stays with me because it represented concretely the power of written words, how they can touch others and net changes for the better. Words can, to use the popular cliche, make a difference. They did so here by humanizing a homeless woman. Many people felt for her and saw that they, too, could be in her place. "There but for the grace of God go I," my Times editor Dick Madden said. Some wealthy women contacted me to say that they never realized how tenuous their comfortable lives were, that they were frightened that if a change of fortune occurred, they might find themselves living in their cars as well.

Response Questions:

1.) Did the article move you to be concerned about this homeless woman, Ans?

2.) What aspects of the story touched you emotionally?

3.) What were the most memorable parts of the story? The most visual?

4.) Give examples of passages where the author shows through his words. Give examples of lines that tell more than show.

5.) What is the story's main point, its thesis?

6.) How would you describe the introduction?

7.) What does this story show about the importance of humanizing your writing?

8.) Could this story have been as effective in choreographing the plight of the homeless without introducing us to Ans or a similar homeless woman? If so, how?

Chapter Seven: Writing About Life-Changing Events

We write to taste life twice, in the moment and in retrospection.

—**Anais Nin**

How does one build that human connection and incorporate it into his or her writing? How do some writers slip into another's shoes so effortlessly, while you wind up bruising your heels? Perhaps it's because these writers have become students of human nature. They have developed empathy for others.

Sometimes such empathy is intuitive due to one's heightened awareness of other people. Other times, empathy stems from one's own self discovery, a discovery leading to emotional truth.

Sounds complex, for sure. Emotional truth? What does it all mean? One of the best ways to ferret out our own emotional truths is to use a power that is yours alone—recall. Recall an experience, an event in your life that had a profound emotional impact on you, one that served as a turning point, one that led to an epiphany of sorts, one that led to growth.

No, this is not an attempt to put you on an analyst's couch, just in front of the keyboard. As stated earlier, nobody knows your life better than you do, and nobody can see the world as you can through your own eyes and your mind's eye.

Memory. It's a powerful resource for a writer, one that can free you up as you begin to search out long forgotten experiences that were important but filed to make room for your busy life.

In this chapter you will practice heightening your own sensitivities through in- and out-of-class assignments that ask you to write via recall about events that greatly changed your life. Perhaps it is a memory from childhood, a time of adult epiphany, or a topic or issue in which you have a strong emotional investment.

Over the years, Norwalk Community College students' recall essays, due to the school's diverse population, have offered me glimpses into worlds no one else has ever seen. There was a middle-aged Peruvian man who wrote about his two-week trek on a mule from his village high in the Andes to Lima. It was there, as an adult, that he saw the ocean for the first time in his life. Then there was the welfare mother who wrote about "being on the orange cord" in her tenement. She explained that the orange cord, a long extension chord, would be plugged into another's apartment when Connecticut Light & Power turned off her electricity. Several essays choreographed the life changing effects of becoming a mother while in high school. And I'll never forget a Mexican woman's essay describing her emotions upon discovering that she was pregnant around the same time she was about to be smuggled across the border by her *coyote*. She described the pain of knowing that her parents, whom she left behind, would never see her child.

These are just a few that stand out in my mind, but there have been literally hundreds over the years that captured my attention, left me thinking, and drove home the point that everyone has a story to tell, everyone has a voice, everyone can write powerful prose via head and heart. Not everyone has to see a new landscape like the Peruvian man or the Mexican woman to tell a good story. Again, they just have to see the world—and their lives—through a different set of eyes.

The following essay is by C. Emma Villavincencio, a woman in my Fall 2007 Composition class at Norwalk Community College. Emma, a native born Brit with impeccable English, exemplified the kind of dread most students feel when setting foot in a required writing class. I could never comprehend her fears since she displayed so much talent. Yet despite such angst, she jumped head first into the recall essay, and before I even read it, she was determined to defend it. "It's how I feel, and I'm not going to change it," she said.

Great, I thought. The power of her own story had surpassed her anxiety about writing. And Emma's was not an isolated case. Over the years, recall essays, usually assigned at the beginning of the semester, always prove to be the most powerful. In fact, when my colleagues and I examine the students' portfolios at the end of each semester, polished recall essays are usually the most memorable. Good ones, like the one below, "All Grown Up," tap into one's unique life experiences, melding logic and emotion into a writing tour de force.

ALL GROWN UP

By C. Emma Villavincencio

An event that occurred in my eleventh year changed my life permanently. Up until that point my childhood had been a fairly happy one. My family was never well off, but there was always plenty of love. I was the oldest of three children, having two younger, boisterous brothers. My dad worked hard but he always made time for us. Even at eleven, I was still daddy's little girl and his attention made me feel special. My mum kept a smoothly run house and took good care of us all. My family life was a stable and fulfilling one. Outside of home, I was a successful student, enjoyed school and had some close friends. Overall, my life was good.

That weekend day in June started off like many others. A lazy morning, my younger brothers and I watching a children's television show. My mum calling out from the kitchen that breakfast was cooking. I remember her standing at the stove frying batches of eggs for us all, toast browning under the grill. My dad was already at the table reading the newspaper. We started eating and my dad, getting up, offered me his unwanted third egg which I eagerly took. He was on his way out to help our friends Keith and Carol move some furniture into their new house. He kissed us all before he left and I will always wish I had said something more than just, "Goodbye."

Later that morning I was pottering around upstairs in my bedroom. I might have been reading or drawing, probably listening to music, leisurely enjoying the day. My mum was in the bathtub and my brothers were most likely out in the garden as I cannot remember hearing their usual noisy rowdiness. I heard a knock at the front door, certainly not uncommon at our house, then a female voice calling "hello." I came to the top of the stairs and found Carol. She was asking where my mum was and I wondered, for a second, why she was not at her new house organizing the furniture. I called my mum but she was already coming out of the bathroom telling Carol to come on upstairs. "I need to talk to your mum," Carol said as she followed her into my mum and dad's bedroom and closed the door. At the time I thought it a little odd that she would shut the door but I guessed they wanted privacy so I went back to my room. A moment later I heard my mum cry out almost as if in pain and I knew something was definitely wrong.

I knocked at the closed bedroom door and Carol opened it. My mum was sitting on the bed, her face pallid. I could tell that Carol was uncomfortable having me there but my mum beckoned to me and I sat beside her. My mum was always very open about everything and she told me that my dad had felt ill while moving our friend's furniture. He had said that his chest hurt and when the pains did not subside, an ambulance had been called. He had been taken to the hospital and Carol had driven directly to our house to tell my mum.

There was a flurry of activity. Carol suggested that they drive to the hospital so my mum who was still wrapped in a towel from her bath, attempted to find clothes. Carol called my nana to come over and stay with my brothers and I. My mum asked her to call my aunt as well. My nana lived just down the street and arrived within minutes. She asked if my mum had called the hospital for an update. Having no experience in situations like this, it had not occurred to my mum or Carol to try that. My nana, as usual, took over the situation. She found the number for the local hospital in the phonebook and after some holding, explaining, and holding again, she eventually hung up.

During this time, I had just been hanging around trying to make sense of this whole thing. My mum seemed quiet and unresponsive, while her friend Carol was somewhat frantic and apologetic. I knew that an ambulance and hospital meant something was wrong with my dad but I just could not fathom what might be wrong. He was just thirty six years old, my strong, wonderful dad. Had he hurt himself while lifting heavy furniture? Had he broken a bone? Surely it could not be any worse than that. I was already worried, but when I saw my nana's face after she hung up the phone, I became alarmed. My nana, never fazed by anything, appeared to be lost for words. She sat my mum down, now clothed but with hair dripping wet, and took her hand. I think my presence in the room was forgotten. My nana told my mum that a man had been brought to the hospital, "dead on arrival" and that she should go and look at the man to see if he was my dad. My mum just stared at her as if she was talking some other language. I understood how she felt. That formation of words, "dead on arrival" was foreign to me also but somehow I knew exactly what it meant.

My aunt had now also arrived and after exchanging some words with my nana she helped my mum out to her car. My brothers must have come back inside at some point because they were playing in the living room. They must have sensed that something was not quite right because they were unusually quiet, almost subdued. They asked where mum was going as my aunt drove her away, but I had no words for them.

I sat looking out of the front window for a long time. I must have gotten up at some point but I do not remember. I know my nana and I talked but I do not know what we might have said. The hospital was not far from my home so I know that my mum could not have been gone that long, but it felt like hours. Those words, "dead on arrival" kept churning through my head. There must have been a mistake. The people at the hospital could not have been talking about my dad. That man must be someone else. My dad had to be okay. He probably had some small injury that we would all laugh about later when he came home. I waited and I prayed with my heart in my mouth.

My heart started to beat very fast when I eventually saw my aunt's car pull into our driveway. It was still early afternoon but it felt so much later. I thought my dad might be in the car with my aunt and my mum, this whole mix up finally cleared away. I could only see two people in the car but I still had hope. Maybe my dad had to stay in the hospital for a few days just like when my brother had his appendix taken out. So many things passing through my mind but I would not let myself think the worst. My aunt got out of the car first and then went around to my mum's side. Why was she helping her out of the car? But then I knew. One look at my mum's tear-stained, ashen face and I knew everything. My father was never coming home.

There were many changes in my life after the death of my father. Some of them, like the way my friends either avoided me or were awkwardly polite, were temporary. At school, I felt as though I had some strange contagious disease but eventually things there went back to normal. Things at home would be forever changed. In the first few weeks there was the general clearing out of clothes and the division of personal items. There always seemed to be a family member coming by with an errand to run or some project to do. I guess they thought if we stayed busy, we would not have time to think about our loss. In some ways this helped, but there was always time to think. Remembering all the good times with my dad was painful, but I never wanted to forget. It is odd how the mind copes with grief. I remember actually laughing at something my cousin did the day after my dad died. Later I felt guilty for feeling a moment of relief and to this day it still astounds me that for that instant, I was able to forget my sorrow. Of course as time passed, the sharp sadness would gradually fade to a dull ache.

My mum changed considerably after she lost her husband. She became withdrawn and helpless. She needed someone to lean on and I took some of that burden. I became an adult in that eleventh year of my life and it has definitely honed who I am today. My cooking and housekeeping skills improved. I learned how to change light bulbs and what tools to use when my brother's bike broke. I disciplined my siblings when necessary and became fiercely protective of them.

That first Christmas Eve on our own, my mum and I shared a glass of brandy while setting out the presents for my brothers to discover the following morning. I felt like a stand-in parent not just in the physical sense but emotionally as well.

I know I would be a different person today if I had not lost my father at such a young age. However, I cannot say I would be a better person. I had to grow up very quickly and I probably missed out on a large part of my childhood, but I am not resentful. I am strong and independent and believe I have my experiences to thank for that. I may not have traveled abroad and eventually found my home and my terrific husband if I had not learned, in my youth, to be self sufficient and to take risks. As for my family, my brothers are now young men and my mum is happily remarried to a loving man. I also now have a sister. I will always love and miss my dad, but I am comfortable with whom I turned out to be, and my life is again happy.

Response Questions:

1.) What is the thesis of "All Grown Up" by C. Emma Villavincencio? Is the thesis clearly stated or implied? Explain.

2.) How does Ms. Villavincencio's life change after her father's death?

3.) Explain what the author means by the following lines: "I know I would be a different person today if I had not lost my father at such a young age. However, I cannot say I would be a better person."

4.) What does this essay tell about the way some people cope with grief? Give examples from the text.

5.) The author writes, "Of course as time passed, the sharp sadness would gradually fade to a dull ache." Does she still feel that "dull ache?"

6.) Do you think it was emotionally grueling for the author to relive these memories, or do you think the distance of years made it easy?

7.) How do you think you would handle writing about distant, painful memories? Give it a try. Think of an event from your past or childhood and write a one-page recollection.

8.) In writing your recall essay, did you become flooded with memories and emotions long forgotten? Did thinking and writing about it give you more clarity about your own life? Do you think it did that for the author of "All Grown Up"?

The following essay, "The Land of the Jaunty," was written by Marcin Cwalina, a Polish man who only began speaking English several years ago. Marcin has worked hard on honing English, his second language, and he doesn't let this challenge prevent him from writing stories when they are close to his heart.

THE LAND OF JAUNTY
By Marcin Cwalina

When one grows up, he or she observes the events that are happening around, and everything can engrave unforgettable memories in one's mind. For me, my childhood was a period of life which I recall with fondness. It included times when I was looking jauntily at life and when I didn't have to worry about anything. That time also included the space were I grew up. All the activities I used to perform and the people who were around me contributed in creating my personality. But there came a time in my life when I had to leave my hometown, and my memories became my treasure which cannot be taken away from me.

I left my country over five years ago, and since then I have been back there three times for short periods. A couple years after I left, my parents moved to a different neighborhood. My older brother and sister moved out of the house a few years before me. This is why my first visits were very strange. I did not feel comfortable. I was getting a feeling like I was in a hotel because it wasn't my old place, my old room, my old view from the window.

My hometown, Lomza, lies in north-eastern Poland and on banks of the Narew River which has so many turns that in one mile of land there are probably four miles of river. My neighborhood was on the south side of the town, and it was built in the years of communism. My parents, sister, brother, and I moved in to one of the new, five story apartment buildings in 1984; I was almost two years old. From what I heard, back then our building was on the border of a growing community and agricultural fields. As the time was going by I was growing along with the housing estate. I remember playing hide and seek on a nearby construction area where the town line was being moved more and more south, into the fields. My friends and I used to play on the playground in the front of the building where our moms could call us when dinner was ready. Hah, eating was one of two reasons that would make us go home, besides going home to go to bed, totally exhausted.

One day, my friend and I were chasing one another, and when making a sudden u-turn, he grabbed one of two branches of a little tree that grew next to the sidewalk outside my room window. The tree split. I remembered from biology class how to deal with this type of situations and I approached to work. I dug out a little bit of wet layer of earth; I put it on the crack and tied the injured tree with a piece of rope. After some period of time the branches were fused. One couple that lived in the same building saw the whole operation. The following spring when the tree blossomed, they complimented me saying that I did a good job. They even dubbed this tree The Marcin Tree; they were very nice neighbors. At this point, I was around ten years old.

This past summer I went to Poland for a few days. During this third visit at my parents', I finally started to feel more at home. I got used to the fact that Wyszynskiego is the street where I will stay each time I go. One of summer I went to see how things were going on Malachowskiego Street, my childhood street. A couple of my friends still live there; one of them is that guy that had broken the tree back in 1990s. While I was waiting for my friend to meet me outside, I enjoyed the view of the slightly changed neighborhood. Some workers were finishing putting new, colored plaster on the outside walls of the building with a huge number 13 and the name of the street on the sides. The playground stayed the same except for a new short fence surrounding the playing field; each section of it painted with a different color. Right next to the fence there was a tall tree, beautiful too, with its branches reaching third floor. Its fat and stable trunk set in covered with grass ground, and its arms, sprinkled with light green leafs, were giving a shade to a nearby bench. This was the tree that I saved. I never realized how fast it was growing when I lived there, but after few years of not seeing it, I was amazed. As I entered my old stairway, I saw a brown door with a black handle that I used to open and close several times a day when I lived there. New owners of the apartment did not even change locks. Paint on the walls was still pistachio green, and writing on one of the steps said "Painted in April, 1998".

My mind was filled with memories of good old days as I was walking around Malachowskiego Street. I know that it all ended because I got older, and I have gotten more responsibilities, not because I have moved to a different country. It is the course of nature that one starts a new episode in his life. Still, we appreciate jaunty living, dinner on the table every day, prepared with a bit of mother's heart in it. It's when we are bustling in this race that our memories gain their value.

Response Questions:

1.) As stated earlier, English is the author's second language. Considering that, how would you rate the job he did in writing this essay? Does it have a thesis? What is it?

2.) The author spends a lot of time writing about a tree. Does this tree provide any symbolism that reinforces the author's thesis? If so, describe its symbolism.

3.) Some might call this a "coming of age" rather than a "coming to America" essay. Why? Explain the significance of the word "jaunty."

The following essay is by another foreign student, Fabiane Cristina Faria-Correa. She hails from Brazil. You will notice that this essay is rich in sentiment and emotion. Still, the emotion does not overshadow the story Fabiane is determined to tell.

BACK TO BRAZIL

By Fabiane Cristina Faria-Correa

Six years have passed since I have seen my father. I can still hear my father's voice pleading, "Please promise me you will come back!" He could already feel what I could not see. I was leaving my country, Brazil, for the first time and heading to New York City for a twenty-day vacation. I guess my father felt in his heart what was to come. I never returned to Brazil until this past summer. Here I was with my bags packed to go back home to visit my father. With me I brought a full load, my husband and daughter. I left as a twenty-one-year-old girl, and I am going back a twenty-seven-year-old wife and mother.

At the airport I could not believe I was really going. My excitement was so great that I could not sleep for days before our trip. My daughter, two years old, was going to meet her grandfather for the first time. He was someone she had always heard about but had never seen. A nine-hour flight followed by another one-hour flight made me feel like the clock moved too slowly. Aline, my daughter, was so excited about the trip that she could not stop talking and moving at the airport and in the plane.

Upon arriving at the final airport in Belo Horizonte, MG at about noon, it looked like there was a party being held in the main lobby. There were about twenty-five people waiting for us to arrive, including my grandparents, my father, uncles, aunts and lots of cousins. It was unbelievable! They were not just waiting for me but waiting to see the new member of the family, the one with brown eyes, hair colored like honey, about two feet tall, slumber like a sleeping beauty. She looked so pretty and so tired. The bags were taking forever to arrive, and there I was, staring at my family through a glass door. My father came closer and when the door opened, I rolled the stroller through the door to his hands. He was crying. The luggage finally arrived and I was able to hug all my loved ones. I do not have enough words to describe those hugs, strong and warm wrapped in tears and smiles.

The ride home was a two-hour drive. We passed by the places that my father had once brought me to so many times, when I was just my daughter's age. I was imagining how it would be to see her playing and running in the same places that I had run and played when I was her age. There were about seven cars driving all together, one behind the other. The two hours rushed by and we arrived at my uncle's house. Why were we going there first? I did not know, until the garage door opened. Surprise! Balloons, a barbecue, and about fifty other family members were waiting for us to arrive at a big party.

Aline woke up as the car stopped. Her eyes were shining; it was the first time she saw that many people staring at her at once. I was afraid of her reaction. All of my family was so excited to look at her, hug her, kiss her and touch her. I thought she would become shy and hide under my legs, but instead she hugged and kissed everybody. She acted like she already knew all of them. She had so much energy that I could not believe it. She loved having so many kids to play with. They all loved her, even though they were meeting her for the first time. I have to admit that the whole arrival party was for her, the new family member. My coming back was a mere detail in all the expectation toward my daughter. For a mother there is nothing else like seeing your child being loved.

Then they saw me, six years older, tired from a trip that so far had lasted for twenty hours. I was excited to see and hug everyone. I had so many hugs and kisses, I felt rejuvenated. I looked at all my loved ones and realized that, just like me, some of my cousins also had babies. The babies that I left behind were now big kids, and the big kids were now teenagers. Some of them I could not recognize right away. My grandparents were now marked even deeper with the lines of suffered years. My father looked older, but happy to see me and thrilled to be holding his first grandchild. It was a new beginning for him. He was not just a grandfather, but the grandfather of an American girl, the only one in the family. And I was no longer Daddy's little girl; my daughter would now play that role. How pleasant it is to have so much love in our lives!

The years had changed everyone, giving some more vigor and mass, giving others more lines and stress. I changed a lot, but still have the same young girl face. My eyes have traveled to so many different places. I have been introduced to so many different cultures. I have seen so much of a world that my family only knows from a TV screen.

Their perceptions of the world had not changed, just like their houses and streets seemed frozen in time. What frustration! I really expected things to be different, but instead they were all the same.

Back at my uncle's farm where I grew up running and playing, I watched my daughter doing the same. Time did not change anything. There were the chicks, the pigs, the cows. And there was Aline running barefoot in the same dust. She fed the animals, picked some eggs from the chickens and went horseback riding. So much fun or a two year old who was raised in an apartment! It was her best time ever!

The two months seemed to go as quickly as ice cream melts. Aline enjoyed the visit so much, and I enjoyed seeing everything through her eyes. I treasured being with my family, saying good night to Daddy, "Benca pai, dorme com Deus!" Most of all I enjoyed hearing his answer, "Deus te abencoe minha filha!"

I can see how much I have changed, and that those beautiful places where I grew up are for visiting and for memories. Living there again is definitely not an option anymore. I will always yearn to visit my loved ones, but I just do not fit in there any longer.

Response Questions:

1.) What part of this essay was the most emotional? Does the author's use of emotions serve to move the essay forward?

2.) Why is it so important for Fabiane Cristina Faria-Correa to see her homeland through her daughter's eyes?

3.) The novelist Thomas Wolfe in *Look Homeward Angel* states that you can never go home again. What does this phrase mean? Does the author of the essay you just read share the same viewpoint? How? Give examples.

4.) Knowing that English is the author's second language, what writing changes might you suggest to make this essay even more powerful?

Remember Brian Coppola who wrote "Lucky Soles" about his combat boots. Here's his memory essay from the front in Iraq. This essay differs from the above compositions in that Brian chose to write about what happened in the third person.

A RANGER'S STORY

By Brian Coppola

Gleaming at his dead and wounded brothers screaming for help, a tear began to roll down his cheek. Blood was everywhere, men were suffering, and soldiers were running around ragged trying to help their injured comrades. The chaos and panic at the hanger that day seemed as if the world was about to end and everyone was running in all different directions. Death and gunpowder was the only thing you were able to smell. The young 20-year-old Ranger had just been in the worst and bloodiest battle of his army career. If he had known about this day, he would have never joined the Army and would have gone off to school instead.

The mission they were on was to take three hours, but instead it turned into two days. It was a simple extraction mission of an Al Qaida operative in southwest Baghdad. The special operations command said that with three platoons, about 75 men, the job would easily be able to be executed. They were not using the regular Army infantry soldiers, they were using Rangers, who were elite soldiers and very professional. The Rangers were to be dropped in by birds three miles away from the extraction point, move to the house, grab the target, and then march to the LZ where they would be picked up by Blackhawks. Everything had gone to plan until they got to the LZ with the prisoner. Their helicopters never came. The fly zone was too hot so they did not want to risk a chance of a bird getting shot down. Now, the rangers had to walk back to base, which was over 15 miles.

Out of the 75 man operation, 37 made it back in one piece, 21 were severely injured, and 17 were still out in the city. Walking back to base they encountered numerous ambushes, insurgents, roadside bombs, and RPG fire. This battle was one of the worst ever to take place in the war in Iraq.

The Rangers, who had no sleep or food in the past 48 hours, were suddenly asked on a volunteer basis, to go right back out to retrieve they're brothers still trapped in the city. The young 20-year-old Ranger from Fairfield, Connecticut was among the men asked to go back out. In his mind it was another suicide mission. Thinking of what he had just gone through and after watching many of his friends get killed, or get injured, he couldn't go out and put himself in harm's way again. Even an elite soldier like a Ranger has limits.

The young man then started thinking about home. He thought about his parents, his sister, and his best friends waiting for him. He even started thinking about his dog, a beautiful German shepherd that he had since he was 15, the most loyal and devoted dog ever. The thought of never seeing home again flashed across his mind, and the thought of dying seemed as real to him as ever now. How could he go out back out there with a 50 percent chance of getting killed or hurt? Would he risk it all to save his brothers who were still trapped in the city?

He then glanced at his friends next to him who were getting geared up and were ready to head back out. The medic station had just asked him if he wanted to get treated for his injuries and if he did, he would be able to go to them. He had a minute to make his decision. This was one of the most important decisions he ever had to make. It wasn't something he would be able to regret later on; it was bigger than that. It was almost life or death. Staring at his troops, he stood up. He could either go join them, put his life in danger again and save his brothers or he could go to the medic station to rest. He began to walk.

Response Questions:

1.) Why do you think the author writes about himself in the third person instead of the first?

2.) What are the conflicts that the Ranger faces externally and internally?

3.) What is the author's personal revelation or adult epiphany, and how does it shape his decision at the end.

Now, I'd like to share with you an adult epiphany I had, one that convinced me after decades of writing that I wanted to teach, too. It also opened my eyes to the enormous role of community colleges and the importance they play in higher education and society. Writing it not only reaffirmed what I believed; it added greater dimension. The following is a chapter from a book I'm finishing up called "Real Class" about my experiences at Norwalk Community College. Here we go:

Real Class

I remember climbing the stairwell, slowly and wondering what kind of impression I would make. From the bottom up I wore Brogs that slipped neatly into the marble steps worn crescent like by years of students running to and from class. I wore dark pants, a brown tweed jacket, a blue button down collar shirt and a red tie my wife had picked out. She had said the tie was the best for now, but that I would need to get some new ones soon.

Professorial was the look I wanted, and I hoped the clothes would help me pull it off since I had never taught before. I had lectured in college classes, mostly at Fairfield University where as a journalist I had been invited to talk to aspiring, eager adult writers in continuing education classes. Or to blase, teenage undergraduates who had seemed more interested in MTV and probably wouldn't have flinched if I had cartwheeled out the window. Each time at Fairfield, I would try to regale them — successfully with the adults and unsuccessfully with the teenagers — with my greatest hits. I'd play portions of the tape from my interview with a serial killer and my sit down with the Imperial Wizard of the Ku Klux Klan. I'd try to impress them with what it was like conducting an interview with armed members of a youth gang in a tenement basement. In short, I was trying to wow them with how cool I was as a reporter. And then I could leave and return the next time one of the professors had to fill his or her slot with someone wanting to feel like a big shot.

But this time it was my class and a full semester's commitment beginning Feb. 8, 1996. I would have to give out assignments, grade tests and papers. I would have to have a plan and be organized. What was Ada Lambert thinking?

She was a cornerstone of Norwalk Community College and the woman who had set up its communications department. She needed someone at the last minute to teach a course.

"Jim, it's Ada Lambert, I remember you from Fairpress, and Joan Antel tells me you've been stringing for the New York Times. I was wondering if you'd like to teach a communications course."

I played the phone message several times. She said something about a 10-week semester, that she had a syllabus I could use and lesson plans. It seemed turn key. I called her back and said yes. The course would pay about $1,900.

What did I have to lose? I was writer first, and I would just be passing through to add another notch on my CV. I felt that teaching a small class was a poor substitute for touching the lives of thousands, even millions of readers with my stories. And this was just a community college, not a revered four-year school where I thought I should be teaching. After all, weren't community colleges bush league schools of last resort, a dumping ground for people who shouldn't be in college in the first place?

I steeled myself that this stint would be even less daunting since this class wasn't even being held on Norwalk Community College's campus, but at night in a Stamford, Connecticut high school. This was Norwalk's "Stamford Campus" with evening classes at West Hill High School.

West Hill High. I thought about it as I stood in the hallway a half hour before the class began. This was the school that members of a gang I had written about 15 years earlier, had attended. And they were upset by my story. Maybe, just maybe, they were adults now, enrolled in my class and still carrying a grudge.

"You the teacher?" asked a young Hispanic man in his 20s.

"Yes, hello."

"I'm Oscar," he said, with a sense of reverence few American students would reserve for the Pope. "Your student."

Oscar was followed by a few men and women in their 20s and a few middle-aged women, black and white. It wasn't long before the class filled to the dozen or so names on the roster. I would write my name on the board, welcome them, hand out the syllabus, ask them to introduce themselves, and ask why they are taking the course. Then I spouted something I had been turning over in my mind since the drive along the Merritt Parkway to class.

"You live in perhaps one of the most exciting times in communication," I said. "You're in the midst of a communications explosion. Every day you hear of something new. From VCRs and CDs to computers to fax machines to now talk about cyberspace and the Internet. It's all around you, and you're on the front lines. The technology is everywhere. What this does is that it behooves you to be better consumers of communication."

I studied their eyes for any sign of interest.

I, of course, was technologically challenged. I had cut my teeth on manual and electric typewriters and in a newsroom with rotary phones and ashtrays on every desk. I had graduated to a word processor and eventually to a computer that to me was merely a typewriter that glowed in the dark. On it I crafted amber colored words I could save on big floppies in a language called Xywrite, which by now might as well have been Sanskrit. I even still read my stories over the phone to the recording room at the New York Times, having to spell out each name, comma, closed quote and paragraph break only to have some exasperated old codger call me back close to midnight to determine whether I said an "s" or an "f."

And now there was all this hype about the Internet, cyberspace and dot-com this and dot-com that. It wasn't even ancient Greek to me because I knew the Greek alphabet. This new stuff was too new, and it kept changing daily. How could something so mercurial and ever changing as high-technology ever measure up to the classics in the communications textbook we'd be using? This text extolled Ptolmey's first library at Alexandria, Guttenberg's press, the Luminere brothers first attempt at moving pictures, the First Amendment, the New York Times, Edward R. Murrow, the tried and true telephone. Internet? We'd see how long it would last.

"I don't get it," I said. "Everyone who's on the Internet, the minute they find out someone else is too, asks, 'What's your email address. I'll email you.' Would you walk up to someone and say, 'You have a phone? So do I. What's your phone number? I'll call you.'"

They snickered. Still, they knew this was the way of the future. I was the dinosaur. The Turn of River Branch of Stamford's Ferguson Library, only a few miles away from West Hill, displayed a flowing banner stating "Come Explore the Internet at the Ferguson."

As the semester moved along the students would educate me.

"It's really great, you can go all over," said Bill, one of my two cyber-savvy students. "You can go into all of these chatrooms where you can type and communicate live with celebrities. I was in a chatroom the other night with Pamela Anderson."

"Ooohh," someone sighed.

"You know, the Baywatch babe," said the white, middle-aged woman from north Stamford.

"Yeah, I know," I shot back.

Oscar extolled how the Internet was great because he could email his parents in Colombia.

"I even put a picture of my daughter on a scanner and emailed it to my parents so they can see her," he said.

Impressed, I knew I had to keep up. Still, there was something too easy about it all. True, the Internet was a great way to exercise First Amendment rights, and the freedom of the press no longer seemed to rest with those who owned the press. The Internet was the new Penny Press, a subject we would cover, and everyone now was an instant publisher. Still, the technology could only take you so far.

"I don't care how good your computer is, it's only as good as what you send over it," I said one night, still wearing the same tie. "Everything begins with our ability write, to articulate our thoughts, to get them down. Everything begins with ideas, with words."

They weren't buying it.

"Okay, you go into Home Depot, and you buy the best saw, a Makita router, a nail gun, a lathe and every other high priced tool like Norm Abrams or Bob Vila has," I said.

There eyes opened.

"And now you're going to take all of this and some of the best lumber to make a terrific flower box." I continued. "But there's just one problem. You don't know basic carpentry. You have no skill at it because you never really worked at it. But someone with just a hand saw and a miter box can make a really great window box because he has the basic skills. They know how to make something. But your window box, with all the high-priced tools you bought at Home Depot, looks like crap."

They got the metaphor. Weeks later we turned to the chapter on newspaper editorials and columns, and I instructed them to think about an issue they felt strongly about and to write about it. For homework, I asked them to scour national and local newspapers to get ideas.

"All the communications out there is for naught unless you can write your ideas down, and to do that you have to write about what you know and to write with your head and your heart."

Now I had them. The next class one woman wanted to write about senseless teen violence. She brought in an article from the Stamford Advocate about 18-year-old Matthew Kosbob who had been beaten with a beer bottle in a city park to the point of brain damage. Matthew, whom I later traveled to Hartford to see when writing a story about him for the Times, would die within a year. On this night, this woman's opinion piece was moving. It expressed all the fury and fear that any mother, any parent, would feel.

Next up was Oscar. He was fired up about the attitude toward immigrants. He had read that then presidential hopeful, commentator Pat Buchanan, wanted to build a wall across the Mexican border to keep illegal immigrants out, a topic that's still an emotional flashpoint in as of this writing in 2008.

"It's based on racism," Oscar insisted. "Nobody's talking about putting a wall across the Canadian border, and they're coming over and taking our $100,000 jobs, not to work for less than minimum wage."

Oscar worked at a Greenwich deli counter slicing meet for well heeled customers to whom he was basically invisible. He felt the racism daily.

By the next class Oscar had penned a powerful essay that covered myriad arguments as to why Americans were more opposed to southern immigration than northern. He worried about some of his word choices and grammar slip ups with Spanish being his first language.

"Don't worry. I'll help you edit that. Just make your point," I told him.

It was the Tuesday after Easter and only a few more classes until the 10-week semester would be over. The students had grown on me as did my feeling about teaching.

"You know what your students are going to get you for your last class," my wife, Christine chimed in as I headed out the door. "A new tie."

Arriving at West Hill that night, the first caress of a spring night greeted me as I walked through the parking lot where the buds were appearing on the trees. The tie notwithstanding, it was a season of new colors.

When I got to the classroom there was the usual staggered arrival of working adults and students stuck in traffic. Oscar came in late, but he was ecstatic, fanning two front sections of the broadsheet Sunday Stamford Advocate and the Sunday Greenwich Time. Both had run his essay as a lead "Letter to the Editor" on Easter Sunday. I never saw anyone as tall as Oscar was at that moment.

"Look, look. My column," he shouted.

"People have been coming up to me at work and asking, 'Oscar, is this you?' " he said. "They treat me differently now."

And from that moment I would see my role in a classroom and at a community college differently, too. Being a writer, a journalist, was still number one for me because that's how for nearly 20 years I was sure I could reach others. But now I saw something more immediate, something that took place via that most primitive and basic of communication technologies, talking face to face.

The night of the last class Oscar said something to me that cinched it, that would make we want to teach again.

"I used to feel that the world was there, and I was here, and that what I thought wouldn't matter," he said waving his arms. "Now, I have a voice. I count."

If only this were a school with more cachet like Fairfield or Yale, I fantasized. After all, since 1979 I had been immersed in Fairfield County snobbery and label conscious elitism. For years I had covered education for Fairpress, a Gannett Fairfield County newspaper. When it came to education, everyone boasted the best schools to the point where the best seemed average. Community colleges? I kept thinking about what William Henry III said in his book, "In Defense of Elitism." He deplored an egalitarian mindset and decried community colleges as an academic wasteland.

Enough said. Norwalk would just be a springboard, I convinced, or rather deceived, myself.

Still, I remembered something that Ada Lambert said that made me see beyond the stereotype.

"Let me tell you, Jim, after you teach in the community college system, you'll never be happier teaching anywhere else," she said.

I felt myself being drawn and resisting at the same time. But the seed was already planted, and it would take root and grow for years to come. This was the real classroom, more fertile and richer beyond anything the elites could imagine.

Response Question:

1.) What is the significance of the title "Real Class," and what is its relationship to the author's preconceived notions?

2.) This essay is as much about self-discovery as it is about debunking stereotypes. Explain.

3.) What was the turning point for the author that made him view teaching differently?

Chapter Eight: Just Imagine . . .

To know is nothing at all; to imagine is everything.

—**Anatole France**

When it comes to writing term papers, research projects, and academic essays of any kind, the last resource you expect to pull you out of the hole—that seemingly bottomless, angst-ridden abyss that widens as deadline looms—is your imagination.

Imagination, you ask? "That's what I use to escape the weight of reality, you know, that pile of books, computer printouts and article photocopies that I have to jam into my blender of a brain to serve up an eight- to 15-page page paper with works cited. Life would be so much easier if I could use my imagination. But I'm writing a history or biology paper, not *Harry Potter* or *Star Wars*. It's a real paper."

Which means? That you surrender your soul and all that goes with it—including your imagination—to follow academic conventions? Hopefully, academic writing isn't merely the printout of information robots who have sorted, sifted, and stylized—not to mention shortchanged themselves and the reader, too.

Formulaic writing, I've found, often fails because something, or rather, someone, is missing—the person behind the prose. True, the information may be all there and appropriately ordered, but the writer seems to have left for the mall.

Where's the person behind the information? The writer's personality which every piece of writing must contain at some level? I don't care if you're writing an encyclopedia entry or a business brief for *Dry and Deadly Statistics* (I used my imagination to come up with that title.) A part of you must come across, and it won't if you put your paper on a very safe—and dull—cruise control.

Again, it's head and heart, and luckily for you, imagination incorporates both. Now, to use it.

The best way to grasp this is to rethink how you view imagination. It's not all fairy tales, fantasy, and fluff. It's an innate faculty that works wonders in nonfiction, in the real world. Why? Because every great piece of rhetoric that changed the world from The *Declaration of Independence* to Rev. Martin Luther King's "I Have a Dream" speech, every invention, and every scientific discovery began with imagining what could be.

To imagine means to be a visionary and a critical thinker, too. It involves examining the facts in front of you, asking what if, what might happen, and what could be if certain actions are not taken. From environmental concerns to planning the cities of tomorrow to areas of discovery in all disciplines, imagination can be a valuable—and ethical—resource when creating powerful nonfiction.

Yes, nonfiction is a discipline that requires you to remain true to the facts. Now here's the dilemma: how do you keep your nonfiction pure and not lose your credibility, crossing over into that literary limbo of fact and fiction I like to call "faction," which only gives others half-truths?

As a journalist, I've always been quite sensitive to this, deploring agenda-driven writers who make the facts fit the stories they want to tell. After all, in an age of CG imagery and virtual reality, the truth is at a premium these days. Won't incorporating imagination be like adding an accelerant to an already raging fire? Possibly. But there's a right way, and you can learn to walk a fine line that empowers your nonfiction while remaining true to facts.

Take a look at the following essay "A Fable for Tomorrow," a chapter from Rachel Carson's Pulitzer Prize winning book *Silent Spring*. See how she does it.

A FABLE FOR TOMORROW
By Rachel Carson

There was once a town in the heart of America where all life seemed to live in harmony with its surroundings. The town lay in the midst of a checkerboard of prosperous farms, with fields of grain and hillsides of orchards where, in spring, white clouds of bloom drifted above the green fields. In autumn, oak and maple and birch set up a blaze of color that flamed and flickered across a backdrop of pines. Then foxes barked in the hills and deer silently crossed the fields, half hidden in the mists of the fall mornings.

Along the roads, laurel, viburnum and alder, great ferns and wild-flowers delighted the traveler's eye through much of the year. Even in winter the road-sides were places of beauty, where countless birds came to feed on the berries and on the seed heads of the dried weeds rising above the snow. The country-side was, in fact, famous for the abundance and variety of its bird life, and when the flood of migrants was pouring through in spring and fall people traveled from great distances to observe them. Others came to fish the streams, which flowed clear and cold out of the hills and contained shady pools where trout lay. So it had been from the days many years ago when the first settlers raised their houses, sank their wells, and built their barns.

Then a strange blight crept over the area and everything began to change. Some evil spell had settled on the community: mysterious maladies swept the flocks of chickens; the cattle and sheep sickened and died. Everywhere was a shadow of death. The farmers spoke of much illness among their families. In the town the doctors had become more and more puzzled by new kinds of sickness appearing among their patients. There had been several sudden and unexplained deaths, not only among adults but even among children, who would be stricken suddenly while at play and die within a few hours.

There was a strange stillness. The birds, for example where had they gone? Many people spoke of them, puzzled and disturbed. The feeding stations in the backyards were deserted. The few birds seen anywhere were moribund; they trembled violently and could not fly. It was a spring without voices. On the mornings that had once throbbed with the dawn chorus of robins, catbirds, doves, jays, wrens, and scores of other bird voices there was now no sound; only silence lay over the fields and woods and marsh.

On the farms the hens brooded, but no chicks hatched. The farmers complained that they were unable to raise any pigs the litters were small and the young survived only a few days. The apple trees were coming into bloom but no bees droned among the blossoms, so there was no pollination and there would be no fruit.

The roadsides, once so attractive, were now lined with browned and withered vegetation as though swept by fire. These, too, were silent, deserted by all living things. Even the streams were now lifeless. Anglers no longer visited them, for all the fish had died.

In the gutters under the eaves and between the shingles of the roofs, a white granular powder still showed a few patches; some weeks before it had fallen like snow upon the roofs and the lawns, the fields and streams.

No witchcraft, no enemy action had silenced the rebirth of new life in this stricken world. The people had done it themselves.

This town does not actually exist, but it might easily have a thousand counterparts in America or elsewhere in the world. I know of no community that has experienced all the misfortunes I describe.

Yet every one of these disasters has actually happened somewhere, and many real communities have already suffered a substantial number of them. A grim specter has crept upon us almost unnoticed, and this imagined tragedy may easily become a stark reality we all shall know.

What has already silenced the voices of spring in countless towns in America? This book is an attempt to explain.

Rachel Carson. from "Silent Spring" (Houghton Mifflin, 1962).

Response Questions:

1.) How does imagination figure into the opening to Carson's book? Does it encourage you to read on?

2.) Does her fairy tale, "Once upon a time" opening sacrifice the credibility of her text? Was it risky, especially since Silent Spring is a very powerful work of nonfiction?

3.) If Carson does not sacrifice her credibility, how does she justify such an imaginary, fictitious opening?

4.) By imagining what could happen if environmental safeguards are not put in place, is Carson being faithful to the truth? Explain.

5.) Search for journal and magazine articles, even books that use similar imaginative devises to drive home their theses? Be prepared to write a brief critical analysis of each? Is it a Carson-type of opening, a composite? You will be amazed at how much imagination is being used to tell perfectly valid nonfiction.

6.) Write a similar five-page essay of your own that employs imagination. Some topics examples might be: a world of alternative energy automobiles, universal healthcare, extended lifespan, genetic engineering, etc. Scour the news for examples and then, just add imagination.

Now, carefully read the classic "I Have a Dream" speech that immortalized Dr. Martin Luther King, Jr. The very fact that King calls it a dream demonstrates that it sprung from his imagination. He imagines a nation free of racial injustice, a vision firmly rooted in the Constitution.

I HAVE A DREAM
By Dr. Martin Luther King, Jr.

I am happy to join with you today in what will go down in history as the greatest demonstration for freedom in the history of our nation.

Five score years ago, a great American, in whose symbolic shadow we stand today, signed the Emancipation Proclamation. This momentous decree came as a great beacon light of hope to millions of Negro slaves who had been seared in the flames of withering injustice. It came as a joyous daybreak to end the long night of their captivity.

But one hundred years later, the Negro still is not free. One hundred years later, the life of the Negro is still sadly crippled by the manacles of segregation and the chains of discrimination. One hundred years later, the Negro lives on a lonely island of poverty in the midst of a vast ocean of material prosperity. One hundred years later, the Negro is still languished in the corners of American society and finds himself an exile in his own land. And so we've come here today to dramatize a shameful condition.

In a sense we've come to our nation's capital to cash a check. When the architects of our republic wrote the magnificent words of the Constitution and the Declaration of Independence, they were signing a promissory note to which every American was to fall heir. This note was a promise that all men, yes, black men as well as white men, would be guaranteed the "unalienable Rights" of "Life, Liberty and the pursuit of Happiness." It is obvious today that America has defaulted on this promissory note, insofar as her citizens of color are concerned. Instead of honoring this sacred obligation, America has given the Negro people a bad check, a check which has come back marked "insufficient funds."

But we refuse to believe that the bank of justice is bankrupt. We refuse to believe that there are insufficient funds in the great vaults of opportunity of this nation. And so, we've come to cash this check, a check that will give us upon demand the riches of freedom and the security of justice.

We have also come to this hallowed spot to remind America of the fierce urgency of Now. This is no time to engage in the luxury of cooling off or to take the tranquilizing drug of gradualism. Now is the time to make real the promises of democracy. Now is the time to rise from the dark and desolate valley of segregation to the sunlit path of racial justice. Now is the time to lift our nation from the quicksands of racial injustice to the solid rock of brotherhood. Now is the time to make justice a reality for all of God's children.

It would be fatal for the nation to overlook the urgency of the moment. This sweltering summer of the Negro's legitimate discontent will not pass until there is an invigorating autumn of freedom and equality. Nineteen sixty-three is not an end, but a beginning. And those who hope that the Negro needed to blow off steam and will now be content will have a rude awakening if the nation returns to business as usual. And there will be neither rest nor tranquility in America until the Negro is granted his citizenship rights. The whirlwinds of revolt will continue to shake the foundations of our nation until the bright day of justice emerges.

But there is something that I must say to my people, who stand on the warm threshold which leads into the palace of justice: In the process of gaining our rightful place, we must not be guilty of wrongful deeds. Let us not seek to satisfy our thirst for freedom by drinking from the cup of bitterness and hatred. We must forever conduct our struggle on the high plane of dignity and discipline. We must not allow our creative protest to degenerate into physical violence. Again and again, we must rise to the majestic heights of meeting physical force with soul force.

The marvelous new militancy which has engulfed the Negro community must not lead us to a distrust of all white people, for many of our white brothers, as evidenced by their presence here today, have come to realize that their destiny is tied up with our destiny. And they have come to realize that their freedom is inextricably bound to our freedom.

We cannot walk alone.

And as we walk, we must make the pledge that we shall always march ahead.

We cannot turn back.

There are those who are asking the devotees of civil rights, "When will you be satisfied?" We can never be satisfied as long as the Negro is the victim of the unspeakable horrors of police brutality. We can never be satisfied as long as our bodies, heavy with the fatigue of travel cannot gain lodging in the motels of the highways and the hotels of the cities. We cannot be satisfied as long as the negro's basic mobility is from a smaller ghetto to a larger one. We can never be satisfied as long as our children are stripped of their self-hood and robbed of their dignity by a sign stating: "For Whites Only." We cannot be satisfied as long as a Negro in Mississippi cannot vote and a Negro in New York believes he has nothing for which to vote. No, no, we are not satisfied, and we will not be satisfied until "justice rolls down like waters, and righteousness like a mighty stream."

I am not unmindful that some of you have come here out of great trials and tribulations. Some of you have come fresh from narrow jail cells. And some of you have come from areas where your quest—quest for freedom left you battered by the storms of persecution and staggered by the winds of police brutality. You have been the veterans of creative suffering. Continue to work with the faith that unearned suffering is redemptive. Go back to Mississippi, go back to Alabama, go back to South Carolina go back to Georgia, go back to Louisiana, go back to the slums and ghettos of our northern cities, knowing that somehow this situation can and will be changed.

Let us not wallow in the valley of despair, I say to you today, my friends.

And so even though we face the difficulties of today and tomorrow, I still have a dream. It is a dream deeply rooted in the American dream.

I have a dream that one day this nation will rise up and live out the true meaning of its creed: "We hold these truths to be self-evident, that all men are created equal."

I have a dream that one day on the red hills of Georgia, the sons of former slaves and the sons of former slave owners will be able to sit down together at the table of brotherhood.

I have a dream that one day even the state of Mississippi, a state sweltering with the heat of injustice, sweltering with the heat of oppression, will be transformed into an oasis of freedom and justice.

I have a dream that my four little children will one day live in a nation where they will not be judged by the color of their skin but by the content of their character.

I have a dream today!

I have a dream that one day, down in Alabama, with its vicious racists, with its governor having his lips dripping with the words of "interposition" and "nullification"—one day right there in Alabama little black boys and black girls will be able to join hands with little white boys and white girls as sisters and brothers.

I have a dream today!

I have a dream that one day every valley shall be exalted, and every hill and mountain shall be made low, the rough places will be made plain, and the crooked places will be made straight; "and the glory of the Lord shall be revealed and all flesh shall see it together."

This is our hope, and this is the faith that I go back to the South with.

With this faith, we will be able to hew out of the mountain of despair a stone of hope. With this faith, we will be able to transform the jangling discords of our nation into a beautiful symphony of brotherhood. With this faith, we will be able to work together, to pray together, to struggle together, to go to jail together, to stand up for freedom together, knowing that we will be free one day.

And this will be the day—this will be the day when all of God's children will be able to sing with new meaning:

My country 'tis of thee, sweet land of liberty, of thee I sing. Land where my fathers died, land of the Pilgrim's pride, From every mountainside, let freedom ring!

And if America is to be a great nation, this must become true.

And so let freedom ring from the prodigious hilltops of New Hampshire.

Let freedom ring from the mighty mountains of New York.

Let freedom ring from the heightening Alleghenies of Pennsylvania.

Let freedom ring from the snow-capped Rockies of Colorado.

Let freedom ring from the curvaceous slopes of California.

But not only that:

Let freedom ring from Stone Mountain of Georgia.

Let freedom ring from Lookout Mountain of Tennessee.

Let freedom ring from every hill and molehill of Mississippi.

From every mountainside, let freedom ring. And when this happens, when we allow freedom ring, when we let it ring from every village and every hamlet, from every state and every city, we will be able to speed up that day when all of God's children, black men and white men, Jews and Gentiles, Protestants and Catholics, will be able to join hands and sing in the words of the old Negro spiritual:

Free at last! Free at last!

Thank God Almighty, we are free at last! (Aug. 28, 1963)

Response Questions:

1.) How many times does King use the word "dream" in his speech? Does the repetition work effectively for you, creating a rhythm, an image, or is it more of an echo effect robbing the word of meaning? Explain.

2.) Is it evident that's King's dream is rooted in the real world, or is it pie-in-the-sky? Explain citing examples.

3.) Many have said that King's rhetoric has the powerful appeal of a sermon. Does it? Do you feel that his background as a minister influenced his choice of words?

4.) In addition to imagination, what about King's use of logic and emotion? Does he write more with his head than his heart? More heart than head? Or, are they properly balanced?

5.) Examine King's use of images, similes, and metaphors. How effective are they. Give examples.

6.) Does King establish his authority from the outset, or, does it develop as the text progresses?

7.) Through research, explain whether or not this speech was a critical turning point in the civil rights movement of the 1960s.

Author's Note: While this text stresses the importance of using imagination and critical thinking as they pertain to nonfiction, it in no way intends to denigrate the importance of fiction and the role it has played throughout the history of civilization. Most of the world's greatest literature, that which have survived millennia, has taken the form of fiction, be it fantasy, composite sketches or even thinly-veiled truth. Fiction, in fact, has propelled humanity forward, entertaining us along the way through its timeless themes that highlight our common humanity, our human condition.

Nonfiction, in most cases, serves a more pragmatic purpose and is often more timely than timeless. That's not to say nonfiction is devoid of powerful themes or that it can never attain the elevated status of literature. On the contrary, it can and does, as Carson and King's writings prove. It's just that the nonfiction writer has to work harder to achieve a work of literature, remaining true to the facts that will guide his or her story. As stated earlier, nonfiction writers can't fudge, bend or alter facts for literary purposes. Even Carson's imaginary introduction eventually comes clean. Remember Rule #4?

So, if you want to write fiction, great. Have fun with it and let your literary talents soar. Just don't try to pass it off as nonfiction or your credibility will suffer.

Come to think of it, I can't think of one reporter I've met who hasn't openly or secretly wanted to pen the Great American Novel. And I've known a number of good, solid journalists who've tried their hand at fiction writing in their off hours. The key is that they knew when to don their fiction hats and when to take them off. And a number of successful authors have been able to do the same so well that their credibility remains beyond reproach. Just Google search one of your favorite authors, and there's a good chance you'll see a breakdown of fiction and nonfiction in their repertoire.

Perhaps writing fiction freed up these authors' imaginations, made them even better nonfiction writers who saw the world differently.

With that said, let's try writing an imaginative essay based on the following two literary works, a short story and a poem. You'll have free range, unencumbered by the real world. The purpose is to exercise your imagination, to stoke your creative process – and to have some fun, too.

Assignments:

Read the following short story "The Lady, or the Tiger" by Frank R. Stockton. A writing prompt follows.

THE LADY, OR THE TIGER

By Frank R. Stockton

In the very olden time there lived a semi-barbaric king, whose ideas, though somewhat polished and sharpened by the progressiveness of distant Latin neighbors, were still large, florid, and untrammeled, as became the half of him which was barbaric. He was a man of exuberant fancy, and, withal, of an authority so irresistible that, at his will, he turned his varied fancies into facts. He was greatly given to self-communing, and, when he and himself agreed upon anything, the thing was done. When every member of his domestic and political systems moved smoothly in its appointed course, his nature was bland and genial; but, whenever there was a little hitch, and some of his orbs got out of their orbits, he was blander and more genial still, for nothing pleased him so much as to make the crooked straight and crush down uneven places.

Among the borrowed notions by which his barbarism had become semified was that of the public arena, in which, by exhibitions of manly and beastly valor, the minds of his subjects were refined and cultured. But even here the exuberant and barbaric fancy asserted itself. The arena of the king was built, not to give the people an opportunity of hearing the rhapsodies of dying gladiators, nor to enable them to view the inevitable conclusion of a conflict between religious opinions and hungry jaws, but for purposes far better adapted to widen and develop the mental energies of the people. This vast amphitheater, with its encircling galleries, its mysterious vaults, and its unseen passages, was an agent of poetic justice, in which crime was punished, or virtue rewarded, by the decrees of an impartial and incorruptible chance.

When a subject was accused of a crime of sufficient importance to interest the king, public notice was given that on an appointed day the fate of the accused person would be decided in the king's arena, a structure which well deserved its name, for, although its form and plan were borrowed from afar, its purpose emanated solely from the brain of this man, who, every barleycorn a king, knew no tradition to which he owed more allegiance than pleased his fancy, and who ingrafted on every adopted form of human thought and action the rich growth of his barbaric idealism.

When all the people had assembled in the galleries, and the king, surrounded by his court, sat high up on his throne of royal state on one side of the arena, he gave a signal, a door beneath him opened, and the accused subject stepped out into the amphitheater. Directly opposite him, on the other side of the enclosed space, were two doors, exactly alike and side by side. It was the duty and the privilege of the person on trial to walk directly to these doors and open one of them. He could open either door he pleased; he was subject to no guidance or influence but that of the aforementioned impartial and incorruptible chance. If he opened the one, there came out of it a hungry tiger, the fiercest and most cruel that could be procured, which immediately sprang upon him and tore him to pieces as a punishment for his guilt. The moment that the case of the criminal was thus decided, doleful iron bells were clanged, great wails went up from the hired mourners posted on the outer rim of the arena, and the vast audience, with bowed heads and downcast hearts, wended slowly their homeward way, mourning greatly that one so young and fair, or so old and respected, should have merited so dire a fate.

But, if the accused person opened the other door, there came forth from it a lady, the most suitable to his years and station that his majesty could select among his fair subjects, and to this lady he was immediately married, as a reward of his innocence. It mattered not that he might already possess a wife and family, or that his affections might be engaged upon an object of his own selection; the king allowed no such subordinate arrangements to interfere with his great scheme of retribution and reward. The exercises, as in the other instance, took place immediately, and in the arena. Another door opened beneath the king, and a priest, followed by a band of choristers, and dancing maidens blowing joyous airs on golden horns and treading an epithalamic measure, advanced to where the pair stood, side by side, and the wedding was promptly and cheerily solemnized. Then the gay brass bells rang forth their merry peals, the people shouted glad hurrahs, and the innocent man, preceded by children strewing flowers on his path, led his bride to his home.

This was the king's semi-barbaric method of administering justice. Its perfect fairness is obvious. The criminal could not know out of which door would come the lady; he opened either he pleased, without having the slightest idea whether, in the next instant, he was to be devoured or married. On some occasions the tiger came out of one door, and on some out of the other. The decisions of this tribunal were not only fair, they were positively determinate: the accused person was instantly punished if he found himself guilty, and, if innocent, he was rewarded on the spot, whether he liked it or not. There was no escape from the judgments of the king's arena.

The institution was a very popular one. When the people gathered together on one of the great trial days, they never knew whether they were to witness a bloody slaughter or a hilarious wedding. This element of uncertainty lent an interest to the occasion which it could not otherwise have attained. Thus, the masses were entertained and pleased, and the thinking part of the community could bring no charge of unfairness against this plan, for did not the accused person have the whole matter in his own hands?

This semi-barbaric king had a daughter as blooming as his most florid fancies, and with a soul as fervent and imperious as his own. As is usual in such cases, she was the apple of his eye, and was loved by him above all humanity. Among his courtiers was a young man of that fineness of blood and lowness of station common to the conventional heroes of romance who love royal maidens. This royal maiden was well satisfied with her lover, for he was handsome and brave to a degree unsurpassed in all this kingdom, and she loved him with an ardor that had enough of barbarism in it to make it exceedingly warm and strong. This love affair moved on happily for many months, until one day the king happened to discover its existence. He did not hesitate nor waver in regard to his duty in the premises. The youth was immediately cast into prison, and a day was appointed for his trial in the king's arena. This, of course, was an especially important occasion, and his majesty, as well as all the people, was greatly interested in the workings and development of this trial. Never before had such a case occurred; never before had a subject dared to love the daughter of the king. In after years such things became commonplace enough, but then they were in no slight degree novel and startling.

The tiger-cages of the kingdom were searched for the most savage and relentless beasts, from which the fiercest monster might be selected for the arena; and the ranks of maiden youth and beauty throughout the land were carefully surveyed by competent judges in order that the young man might have a fitting bride in case fate did not determine for him a different destiny. Of course, everybody knew that the deed with which the accused was charged had been done. He had loved the princess, and neither he, she, nor any one else, thought of denying the fact; but the king would not think of allowing any fact of this kind to interfere with the workings of the tribunal, in which he took such great delight and satisfaction. No matter how the affair turned out, the youth would be disposed of, and the king would take an aesthetic pleasure in watching the course of events, which would determine whether or not the young man had done wrong in allowing himself to love the princess.

The appointed day arrived. From far and near the people gathered, and thronged the great galleries of the arena, and crowds, unable to gain admittance, massed themselves against its outside walls. The king and his court were in their places, opposite the twin doors, those fateful portals, so terrible in their similarity.

All was ready. The signal was given. A door beneath the royal party opened, and the lover of the princess walked into the arena. Tall, beautiful, fair, his appearance was greeted with a low hum of admiration and anxiety. Half the audience had not known so grand a youth had lived among them. No wonder the princess loved him! What a terrible thing for him to be there!

As the youth advanced into the arena he turned, as the custom was, to bow to the king, but he did not think at all of that royal personage. His eyes were fixed upon the princess, who sat to the right of her father. Had it not been for the moiety of barbarism in her nature it is probable that lady would not have been there, but her intense and fervid soul would not allow her to be absent on an occasion in which she was so terribly interested. From the moment that the decree had gone forth that her lover should decide his fate in the king's arena, she had thought of nothing, night or day, but this great event and the various subjects connected with it. Possessed of more power, influence, and force of character than any one who had ever before been interested in such a case, she had done what no other person had done—she had possessed herself of the secret of the doors. She knew in which of the two rooms, that lay behind those doors, stood the cage of the tiger, with its open front, and in which waited the lady. Through these thick doors, heavily curtained with skins on the inside, it was impossible that any noise or suggestion should come from within to the person who should approach to raise the latch of one of them. But gold, and the power of a woman's will, had brought the secret to the princess.

And not only did she know in which room stood the lady ready to emerge, all blushing and radiant, should her door be opened, but she knew who the lady was. It was one of the fairest and loveliest of the damsels of the court who had been selected as the reward of the accused youth, should he be proved innocent of the crime of aspiring to one so far above him; and the princess hated her. Often had she seen, or imagined that she had seen, this fair creature throwing glances of admiration upon the person of her lover, and sometimes she thought these glances were perceived, and even returned. Now and then she had seen them talking together; it was but for a moment or two, but much can be said in a brief space; it may have been on most unimportant topics, but how could she know that? The girl was lovely, but she had dared to raise her eyes to the loved one of the princess; and, with all the intensity of the savage blood transmitted to her through long lines of wholly barbaric ancestors, she hated the woman who blushed and trembled behind that silent door.

When her lover turned and looked at her, and his eye met hers as she sat there, paler and whiter than any one in the vast ocean of anxious faces about her, he saw, by that power of quick perception which is given to those whose souls are one, that she knew behind which door crouched the tiger, and behind which stood the lady. He had expected her to know it. He understood her nature, and his soul was assured that she would never rest until she had made plain to herself this thing, hidden to all other lookers-on, even to the king. The only hope for the youth in which there was any element of certainty was based upon the success of the princess in discovering this mystery; and the moment he looked upon her, he saw she had succeeded, as in his soul he knew she would succeed.

Then it was that his quick and anxious glance asked the question: "Which?" It was as plain to her as if he shouted it from where he stood. There was not an instant to be lost. The question was asked in a flash; it must be answered in another.

Her right arm lay on the cushioned parapet before her. She raised her hand, and made a slight, quick movement toward the right. No one but her lover saw her. Every eye but his was fixed on the man in the arena.

He turned, and with a firm and rapid step he walked across the empty space. Every heart stopped beating, every breath was held, every eye was fixed immovably upon that man. Without the slightest hesitation, he went to the door on the right, and opened it.

Now, the point of the story is this: Did the tiger come out of that door, or did the lady?

The more we reflect upon this question, the harder it is to answer. It involves a study of the human heart which leads us through devious mazes of passion, out of which it is difficult to find our way. Think of it, fair reader, not as if the decision of the question depended upon yourself, but upon that hot-blooded, semi-barbaric princess, her soul at a white heat beneath the combined fires of despair and jealousy. She had lost him, but who should have him?

How often, in her waking hours and in her dreams, had she started in wild horror, and covered her face with her hands as she thought of her lover opening the door on the other side of which waited the cruel fangs of the tiger!

But how much oftener had she seen him at the other door! How in her grievous reveries had she gnashed her teeth, and torn her hair, when she saw his start of rapturous delight as he opened the door of the lady! How her soul had burned in agony when she had seen him rush to meet that woman, with her flushing cheek and sparkling eye of triumph; when she had seen him lead her forth, his whole frame kindled with the joy of recovered life; when she had heard the glad shouts from the multitude, and the wild ringing of the happy bells; when she had seen the priest, with his joyous followers, advance to the couple, and make them man and wife before her very eyes; and when she had seen them walk away together upon their path of flowers, followed by the tremendous shouts of the hilarious multitude, in which her one despairing shriek was lost and drowned!

Would it not be better for him to die at once, and go to wait for her in the blessed regions of semi-barbaric futurity?

And yet, that awful tiger, those shrieks, that blood!

Her decision had been indicated in an instant, but it had been made after days and nights of anguished deliberation. She had known she would be asked, she had decided what she would answer, and, without the slightest hesitation, she had moved her hand to the right.

The question of her decision is one not to be lightly considered, and it is not for me to presume to set myself up as the one person able to answer it. And so I leave it with all of you: Which came out of the opened door—the lady, or the tiger? (1882)

Response Questions and Assignment:

1.) Why do you think the author leaves this story open-ended? How does it compare to today's high-tech mysteries and stories that ask you to come up with your own endings? Based on your research about the story, was Stockton ahead of his time, or was this a common practice to engage readers, to make short stories, literature, an interactive pursuit?

2.) Finish the story. Which one was it, the lady or the tiger? Following the story line maintaining the same tone of the piece – and using your imagination—write a two-page conclusion to this question that has baffled readers for more than a century.

Poem: Now read the following poem by Edwin Arlington Robinson, another work that asks you, the reader, to use your imagination along with your critical thinking skills.

RICHARD COREY

By Edwin Arlington Robinson

Whenever Richard Corey went down town,
We people on the pavement looked at him:
He was a gentleman from sole to crown,
Clean favored, and imperially slim.

And he was always quietly arrayed,
And he was always human when he talked;
But still he fluttered pulses when he said,
"Good-morning," and he glittered when he walked.

And he was rich — yes, richer than a king,
And admirably schooled in every grace:
In fine, we thought that he was everything
To make us wish that we were in his place.

So on we worked, and waited for the light,
And went without the meat, and cursed the bread;
And Richard Corey, one calm summer night,
Went home and put a bullet through his head. (1896)

Response Questions and Assignment:

1.) What type of man is Richard Corey? In what type of community does he live?

2.) What do you think is the poem's theme, the message it drives home?

3.) How are you left feeling at the end of the poem? What was your initial reaction?

4.) White a two-to three-page imaginative essay explaining why Richard Corey took his life. You may set it in any time or place. Don't be shy. Let your imagination run wild. In the past this prompt has elicited some of the most creative and outrageous responses, offering every reason from Richard Corey being a drug lord to a frustrated cross dresser to having lost his fortune at a casino to being a split personality who had to stop his murderous alter ego. One student even made a pretty good case that Richard Corey was actually murdered, and it was made to look like suicide. I mention these to underscore that anything goes in this exercise. Be creative and have fun.

Chapter Nine: Writing Powerful Introductions

If you start with a bang, you won't end with a whimper.
—T.S. Eliot

A s I walked from the kitchen to the living room, searching for another section of the paper, the television blared like background noise, a noise to which I've grown accustomed to turning a deaf ear. My children, having left the TV for a stint with Legos, relinquished the remote to my wife who changed to "Sunday Morning" with host Charles Osgood. Even the congenial, avuncular voice of good old Osgood, whom I had grown to like, couldn't grab my attention this morning. Selective perception allowed me to tune him out, too.

For a second or so my ears pricked up when he mentioned a bestselling author, but it wasn't enough to make me put down the paper. Then I heard some words being read. I don't remember if Osgood or the author were reading. It didn't matter. The words did.

"My father and mother should have stayed in New York where they were married and where I was born. Instead, they returned to Ireland when I was four, my brother, Malachy, three, the twins, Oliver and Eugene, barely one, and my sister Margaret, dead and gone.

"When I look back on my childhood I wonder how I survived at all. It was, of course, a miserable childhood; the happy childhood is hardly worth your while. Worse than the ordinary miserable childhood is the miserable Irish childhood, and worse yet is the miserable Irish Catholic childhood.

"People everywhere brag and whimper about the woes of their early years, but nothing can compare to the Irish version: the poverty; the shiftless loquacious alcoholic father; the pious defeated mother moaning by the fire; pompous priests; bullying schoolmates; the English and the terrible things they did to us for eight hundred long years.

"Above all—we were wet."

Though I'm not impulsive, I had to have that book. The opening paragraphs hooked me, and I wanted to know more about the author, a high school English teacher, whose prose would transform him into a multi-millionaire. Needless to say, I rushed out to add to Frank McCourt's coffers by purchasing his memoir, *Angela's Ashes*. Months later I relayed that story to McCourt when I interviewed him for the *Connecticut Post* at Barnes & Noble's in Westport, Connecticut shortly after he won the Pulitzer Prize for memoir writing.

I retell it now to show the importance of powerful introductions. Without one, your story will get off to a slow start, and if it's too slow, drab even, your readers will quickly lose interest. A great introduction is like a great first impression. People will stick around.

True, first impressions can be deceiving, but any writer who's worth his or her craft will make good on their opening lines, riveting a reader all the way to the finish, one that will leave the reader thinking.

So, how do you start, how do you grab the reader's attention in this age rife with distractions? I refer you back to Rule Number One: You can't be a good writer unless you're a good reader. Pore over introduction to popular books, the classics especially.

It was the best of times, it was the worst of times, it was the age of wisdom, it was the age of foolishness, it was the epoch of belief, it was the epoch of incredulity, it was the season of Light, it was the season of Darkness, it was the spring of hope, it was the winter of despair.

These opening lines of *A Tale of Two Cities* show that Charles Dickens, despite his reputation and loyal following of readers, didn't take his audience for granted.

The cold passed reluctantly from the earth, and the retiring fogs revealed an army stretched out on the hills, resting.

This opening sentence of Stephen Crane's *The Red Badge of Courage* paints a picture that would take a skilled artist days and cost a Hollywood producer millions. They're resting now, but something's bound to happen. You think? The reader wants to know more.

He was born with a gift of laughter and a sense that the world was mad.

Okay, I want to read on. What does Raphael Sabatini have in store for me with *Scaramouche*?

Perhaps my favorite opening line isn't even in English: *Nel mezzo del cammin di nostra vita mi ritrovai per una selva oscura ché la diritta via era smarrita.* Translation: *Midway upon the journey of our life I found myself within a forest dark, for the straightforward pathway had been lost.*

With these opening lines to *Inferno*, the first book of *The Divine Comedy*, 14th Century Florentine poet Dante Alighieri knew how to entice readers, something that still holds today regardless the language into which his work is translated. And talk about head and heart, nothing seems to match Dante's lovelorn obsession with his departed Beatrice as he searches for her in the afterlife.

Okay, by now you might be thinking, "That's great for great books, but isn't this composition—a nonfiction class at that?"

Yes, but the same rule holds true regardless of the genre. You need a great introduction because without one, your writing will fall flat, die even. And getting a reader's attention is a lot more difficult today than when Dante wrote, or even when *Angela's Ashes* was first published in 1996.

Why? Look at today's audience, our busy culture. From cell phones to text messaging to job demands to keeping up with technology to worrying about bills or the price of oil, even having to pump your own gas, people are too distracted now. And when you add to our hurried and harried lifestyles a cultural mindset that espouses "been there, done that," it's no wonder people bore easily. The virtue of patience, it's sad to say, was among the first casualties of the high-tech boom.

So, if you bore the reader—especially at the beginning—he or she turns the page, scrolls down, clicks elsewhere or glances at their cell phone to check messages.

But with a great introduction, one that promises a great read, readers will make the time. Not to sound professionally biased, but this is something newspaper people have known for a long time.

We call them leads (spelled *ledes* in journalese), the few opening lines that are veritable sales pitches to get readers to choose your story.

Back in the late 1970s, the late Joe Ungaro, then executive editor of the Gannett-Westchester Rockland Newspapers, wrote a weekly column titled "Ledes That Caught My Eye" in the newsletter that circulated among staffers. The column praised the week's ledes, those powerful, clever introductions that yanked readers into stories.

Having your lede cited in Joe's column made many a reporter's chest swell with pride. And it made those not mentioned want to work harder to write more captivating introductions.

From a business standpoint, at a time of competition from other print and electronic media, good ledes made good sense. Riveted readers meant happy advertisers and even happier Gannett higher-ups.

And from a rhetorical standpoint, good lede writing was pure magic, perhaps because it was the most audience conscious exercise in writing.

As a Gannett reporter for the chain's only Connecticut paper, *Fairpress*, I wanted to write the best ledes I could, and not just to be mentioned in Joe's column. I sincerely believed that good ledes were everything when it came to being noticed by readers.

"For a man who has more than 100 rabbits' feet, Ted Coley hasn't had too much luck lately."

That was the opening line to a story I wrote about a Connecticut man whose livelihood, raising and selling rabbits, was about to come to an end due to town ordinance prohibiting the sale of fur-bearing animals. And, *ahem*, it made Joe's column.

And it isn't just clever ledes, but great anecdotes and scene setters that set the tone for a story that also prove powerful. Each time I've written a news or feature story, and there have been several thousands of them over the years, it's always the lede that gets my creative juices going.

In short, the lede has always been my contract with the reader, and I always want to make it as best as possible, regardless of whether or not the story was earthshattering.

As I begin to search for examples to share, I discover that keeping a cluttered computer desktop has its advantages. A lot of the stories I've written and sent to the Stamford, Connecticut Advocate over the past three years are still there. Here are some examples:

WESTPORT–Many of his old shipmates are gone, passing like the estimated 2,000 World War II veterans said to die each day. Edward J. Keehan worries that with them a reverence for Pearl Harbor Day will fade, too.

"I think people have lost interest," said Keehan, 83, about Dec. 7, 1941, the day that was to live in infamy. "I think they've even lost interest in 9–11, myself. I can't explain it."

Both dates, however, carry special meaning for Keehan and are showcased in Navy veteran's forthcoming second book, "Memories of Life."

This was the opening to a story about how Pearl Harbor Day was losing, sadly, its significance to a younger generation that considered it ancient history. This story could only be told through the eyes of a World War II veteran who lived through it, and it conveys a lot of emotion from the start.

NORWALK–On a blustery Saturday morning, Anthony Barber stared down the fairway of the fourteenth hole and studied the lay of the land. He saw that the ground dipped and that there was stand of cedar trees in the way.

"I don't know whether I should air this or roll it," said Barber as he took out his driver.

He took aim, and then with a golf stroke more out of Ancient Greece than Edinburgh, he threw his plastic disc, a smaller version of the popular Frisbee, down the 335-foot fairway. The disc curved down toward the ground, just like he wanted, rolled along the hard ground beneath the trees them to make a clear path toward the hole. The hole in this case was an above ground metal basket on a pole, its top draped with chains to deflect the "putter" disc into the basket.

This was the lede to a feature story on disc golf, a sport which is still unfamiliar to many. An anecdotal lede that described the game seemed like a good way to go, yet at the same time I felt the need to play off the golf imagery, setting it up as a typical game of golf and quickly following with an element of surprise.

GREENWICH – Forget buckshot when it comes to controlling the Canada geese population. The weapon of choice in this Gold Coast town can be found in most pantries – corn oil.

In fact, corn oil toting volunteers wiped out about 750 geese here last year based on estimates from the Conservation Commission. They did so by attacking the problem at its source – the egg – as Denise Savageau, conservation director, explains.

The process involves ferreting out nests and rubbing corn oil on the eggs. The porous eggs get suffocated by the oil which prevents an embryo from developing, she said. By the time an unaware mother goose realizes the eggs won't hatch, the nesting season, which runs until the end of June, is over.

This was a story about egg oiling to limit the geese population, an odd story indeed. So, the lede attempts to grab readers by playing on a hunting theme with corn oil, no less.

STAMFORD – One timeworn American Flag had been with Gen. Patton's division in Germany during World War II. The other had flown over the fallen Taliban headquarters in Kandahar, Afghanistan.

And Wednesday morning both banners took center stage at the Holy Spirit Roman Catholic School gymnasium here in a ceremony honoring sacrifice and courage that spanned generations. It was all part of the school's "Character, Compassion and Values" theme highlighted during Catholic Schools Week.

This lede is a scene setter, designed to put the readers there with the image of both flags and their individual places in history.

ROWAYTON – A frosty wind gave a shrill whistle as it whipped through the aluminum mast of Annie Walsh's small sailboat as she readied for the race.

"It's named Zamboni, isn't that great?" she said of her nine-foot sailing dinghy named after the vehicle that polishes ice rinks.

The appellation she gave her craft couldn't have been more appropriate. Ice floes surrounded the floating dock at the Norwalk Yacht Club (NYC) here Sunday afternoon as Walsh and three other diehard frostbite sailors prepared for two hours of races.

Not only does this opening set the scene of a winter day, but it relies upon a powerful Zamboni quote that compares this type of sailing to being on an ice rink.

RIDGEFIELD—At times Victor Demasi seemed like a showman, such as when he took butterfly he had just swooped up with his gossamer net and placed on the tip of eight-year-old Giles Ruck's nose. He joked that Giles would have to stay there all day until the Cabbage butterfly decided to leave. Luckily for Giles, the winged insect in short while took flight.

Other times, DiMasi seemed like a pitchman, hawking the new, first-of-a-kind "Connecticut Butterfly Atlas," on sale for $22 from the state Department of Environmental Protection, a text in which he had contributed more than 1,000 of the 9,000 entries of butterflies in the state.

DeMasi is a professional lepitopterist, a butterfly scientist who has traveled the world studying the elusive, colorful creatures. And he's also a research associate on the subject at Yale University's Peabody Museum.

But for the most part Saturday morning as he walked the Norwalk River Nature Study Area on the Ridgefield-Redding border here, DiMasi came across as just a good humored, regular guy with a life's passion for winged beauty.

Again, here's a news/feature story that would make most hard-bitten news hounds wince at the thought of covering it. A butterfly walk? Yes, but maybe there's no such thing as a dull story, just dull writers. It's the little things and the subtle things about DeMasi's actions and his enthusiasm about butterflies that make this story work, and the lede does a good job setting it up.

BRANCHVILLE—The old antiques shed, a funky, pink landmark for years in this section of Ridgefield on Route 7 here, now sits like an damaged, old scow half submerged in the Norwalk River. It's been there since mid-April.

That was when furious rains and overflowing banks lifted the shed straddling the narrow waterway from the cinderblocks that held it in place for decades, shoving it downstream more than 50 feet. Another hundred and it would have wound up in Wilton, as did some of the antiques.

This is the lede to a story about a small building that had been sitting in the middle of the Norwalk River for more than two months.

It sets up the story by describing how it looks and how it got there. Anyone unfamiliar with the site of it would want to read more.

NORWALK—As he looked out at the veterans, Junior ROTC students, city officials and citizens that filled the Norwalk Concert Hall, Jake McNiece mused from the podium as to why he was there.

"I'm here simply because they wanted to see the bad along with the good," said McNeice., a hell-raising, World War II paratrooper whose antics and adventures inspired the 1968 Lee Marvin movie, "The Dirty Dozen."

Again, a powerful quote shores up the first line, giving the reader a full sense of who, what, when, where, and why.

NORWALK—The Denver Broncos creamed the Atlanta Falcons Monday night 20 to 0, but diehard Falcon fans need not grieve. The game, as realistic as it comes, was played out on a 42-inch screen TV, the players just two local teens working joysticks and buttons in a video game poised to redefine Monday Night Football.

And it all took place at the Norwalk Public Library's ETC, the Extraordinary Teen Center, a safe haven where the real goal is to build a bridge between video and computer games to the world of books.

This is a "things are not as they seem" lede, setting up a premise and quickly letting readers know it's not the case. This contrast creates drama to entice readers.

SOUTH NORWALK—The somber wail of bagpipes warming up matched the mood set by drizzly, dark skies above police headquarters Friday morning here as scores of city officials, family members and officers gathered for the 12th Annual Police Memorial Services.

Again this is a scene setter where a description of the weather matches perfectly with the solemn, sorrowful mood.

All of these examples, from opening lines to good books to news story ledes, underscore the importance of the introduction to all forms of writing. Again, it's your sales pitch. You have to attract the reader by promising a good read—and you have to deliver.

How? By following through. And following through becomes a lot easier after you have an introduction that excites you, too.

True, there are some writers who like to get everything out of the way first and tack the introduction on at the end—what some might call the proverbial icing on the cake.

But I'm not one of those writers. If I have all my research and an outline, written or mental, of what I want to say, the good introduction takes me on the right course. That's because a good introduction, while an important sales pitch for your story, is more than just bait. It's a synthesis of your thought processes on what you are about to write. It's a head and heart declaration, a pledge that you fully comprehend, appreciate, and are excited about your essay, article, or story. Remember Rule Number 2? Good writing is the result of good thinking. Really great introductions are the result of good thinking too, thinking backed up by authority on what you are going to say, organization, sequence, and flow.

So how do you begin your essay? Anecdote? Scene setter? Quote? A straight forward approach with your thesis as the first sentence? Unbelievable statistics? It all depends on what works best—as you see it. The key is to make it the best introduction possible.

When it comes to writing compositions, particularly research essays, I always ask students after they have done most of the research to support their thesis statements, to write introductions for the next class, introductions they will read aloud. Student input—audience input—always proves invaluable. And why not? You're writing for an audience, in this case your professor and your peers, and hopefully an even greater one.

Writers of good introductions understand their audiences better than those who pen mediocre ones. And knowing your audience is key to good writing.

Ah, the audience! What about the audience?

"I have often asked myself: would I still write today if they told me that tomorrow a cosmic catastrophe would destroy the universe, so that no one could read what I wrote today?" asks famed Italian intellectual Umberto Eco, a professor of semiotics at the University of Bologna, at the conclusion of his book *On Literature.*

"My first instinct is to reply no. Why write if no one will read me? My second instinct is to say yes, but only because I cherish the desperate hope that, amid the galactic catastrophe, some star might survive, and in the future someone might decipher my signs. In that case writing, even on the eve of the Apocalypse, would still make sense.

"One writes only for a reader. Whoever says he writes only for himself is not necessarily lying. It is just that he is frighteningly atheistic. Even from a rigorously secular point of view.

"Unhappy and desperate the writer who cannot address a future reader."

Chapter Ten: Tackling the Research Paper

Of all the writing assignments students face, especially in rhetoric or composition classes, none generates as much angst as the research paper. As a rule, it's the one students fear most.

The reasons, naturally, are understandable. In our minds research papers exist on that psychological plane of tests, final exams, and painstakingly tedious papers you've sweated through, the ones that ruined weekends. And then there were those merciless teachers with red pens and power complexes.

Not only that, research papers were usually the ones instructors gave you some time to complete. And students, just like many professional writers, human nature being what it is, tend to procrastinate when it comes to long-term projects.

"I'll do it later," "I have time," or, "I do well under pressure," are among the many mind games you'll play.

Such stalling, however, instead of making things better, kicks up an undercurrent of anxiety, an anxiety that makes the paper seem larger than life. And the research paper soon takes on mythic proportions.

When you procrastinate you're really saying, "I'm going to postpone the pain as long as possible," or, "I'll sweat and suffer later. Just leave me alone now."

All this self-deception and subsequent red ink, give research papers a bad rep. That's not to say they're easy, but they're not the bogeyman of academic life either. A lot of the fear has been hyped, if not by you, by anxious classmates and by academic culture overall.

But in fact, research is simply research, and you've been researching this world ever since your eyes first opened, from finding your mother's breast to walking to learning to drive to deciding how your dress to what movie to see to choosing a college.

You are also part of a generation that literally has the world at your fingertips. Everything you want to know, it seems, is just a mouse click away. How times have changed.

I recall a college research paper that required a trip to New York City's Public Library on 42nd Street, thumbing through the drawers of card

103

listings, finally finding the titles I wanted, writing down the books' numbers in pencil on a piece of paper and handing it to someone at a dumb-waiter. And I'd wait while the cryptic slip descended into the basement where rumors had it researchers on roller skates would navigate through a maze of cavernous aisles to retrieve the texts. Then they would place them on the dumbwaiter so they would arrive above ground. There was only one catch. I couldn't take the texts with me. I'd have to write down what I needed, accurately, of course, or I could use the photocopier. And what a photocopier it was. The copy came out wet, looked like a negative, and had this crummy chemical smell.

When I retell this to students, they snicker. They say I'm from another century. Actually, I am, and at this writing I'm sure they are, too. It's just that to a generation that grew up with computer technology, young people who use their cell phones to pull games out of thin air when they're bored, the story I recounted sounds so Pony Express.

To be clear, I'm not eschewing technology. It's an amazing tool when it comes to research. It's just that not everything you need to know, everything that can be researched, exists out in cyberspace. In fact, the only reason it got to cyberspace in the first place was that some-one did the initial grunt work. What are two words that come to mind? Shoe leather. That means personally getting up from your keyboard, even wearing out your soles and heels, to retrieve information.

Maybe it takes the form of ferreting out texts, journals, and clippings and assorted hard copy that has yet to have been loaded electronically. Or maybe it involves actually interviewing people, experts and other individuals. As a journalist, I always found the interview to be the most intriguing because often it involves breaking new ground.

Let's start by asking why you're writing the research paper in the first place. Okay, it was assigned, but beyond that you're researching to prove your point, your thesis. I always assign research papers in con-junction with an argumentation paper. I want students to take a stand, not just to relay information. The latter, of course, is suited for, demanded, even in journalism class where students are asked to be fair and objective.

But composition and rhetoric classes aim to have you be more than just an informer. You're not writing an encyclopedia entry. Your essays should be thesis driven, and your research gathered from multiple sources serves to support this main point.

Remember the letter to the editor you wrote, or that blog? It's the same idea. Only now you're going to build a case for your argument by researching authoritative sources. How? It's an involved process, but it is manageable and interesting once you get started. In fact, finding information to support your point and disprove counterpoints can be invigorating.

The operative word is sources, and when it comes to sources there are two kinds: primary and secondary.

The primary source is what some used to call, "from the horse's mouth," interviewing experts as opposed to reading what others have to say about him or her. A primary source is the novel itself, not some scholar's literary criticism. It's the movie, the play, not what some reviewer has to say. It's the survey that's been taken, not some analyst's interpretation. It's the president's State of the Union address, not what talking-head commentators have to say about it. And so on.

For beginning writers the thought of using primary sources may seem daunting. Interview an authority, a political leader, a university official? Yeah, right, you say.

But it need not be as difficult as it sounds. Perhaps there is an upcoming lecture or discussion on campus, at your local library, or at the community center where an expert in your area of study will be speaking. Go to the event and jot down what they and others have to say.

If you are hesitant about arranging a face-to-face interview with an expert, try sending him or her an email. While not as complete as in-person, or even phone interviews, email interviews are still good primary sources, ones in which there's little room for misquoting.

Your personal observations also provide great primary source input to your research paper. Describing a scene is the kind of primary source information that every good reporter incorporates.

Some students even opt to use surveys in their research, though my experience has found these surveys tend to be less than scientific. Let's face it, an informal poll taken in the cafeteria or in the quad on what students think about health care, foreign policy, or the lineup of presidential candidates can be fraught with questions of reliability. Unless you're majoring in statistics and have polling experience, I suggest you pass on this one. Remember, you want to build authority and credibility.

Secondary sources, as you know from years as a student, are often easier to access. They are, in short, second-hand information. They include everything from criticisms to commentaries to recycled news reports.

For example, there's a report in the prestigious *New England Journal of Medicine* about a new diabetes treatment. The actual report is a primary one, but barring *NEJM* subscribers, few will actually read the primary source. They will get their information second hand by reading about it in the *New York Times, USA Today* or the *Wall Street Journal*. True, there will be excerpts from the original story, but your sources are still secondary ones. Some gatekeeper has already decided what you should know.

Often, and this is the unfortunate part about the ease in which we use search engines, students tend only to use secondary sources. True, they are perfectly legitimate, though I feel every research paper should include some primary sources.

The important caveats to keep in mind when using secondary sources are these: make sure you use authoritative, not apocryphal ones, and always, always give credit where credit is due via in-text citations. Both of these are critical to the ethos of your piece, your credibility.

Let's begin with the first caveat—using authoritative sources. Understand that not all secondary sources are credible.

If the *New York Times, USA Today,* or the *Wall Street Journal,* to name a few authoritative publications, were to run front page stories that space aliens landed in Washington, D.C. and met with the president who invited them to Camp David for the weekend, would you believe them? I would because these papers' time-honored reputation for reporting. Meanwhile, I'm sure you've seen countless stories comparable to the fictitious one just described as you wait at the supermarket checkout. Those sensational tabloids known for outrageous fabrication run stories like this all the time. Do you believe them? No, or at least I hope not. Most people just laugh or shake their heads.

Okay, that's an extreme example, but in an age or chat rooms, internet hoaxes, and dot-coms with vested financial interests coloring the information presented, it behooves you to critically analyze the information you gather.

For example, let's say your thesis stresses the need for young adults to use cholesterol-lowering drugs to stave off heart attacks later in life. Online you find a site stating, "LIPITOR is clinically proven to reduce the risk of heart attack and stroke in patients with multiple risk factors for heart disease, including family history, high blood pressure, age, low HDL ("good" cholesterol) or smoking." You decide to include it in your paper. There's just one problem. The online source was the official LIPITOR Web-site. The maker of LIPITOR, Pfizer, has a vested financial interest in touting their product's benefits.

Should you use this information? Probably not. If your aim is to support your thesis with the most authoritative sources, avoid those who are out to make a buck. Groups like the American Heart Association or the American Medical Association would offer more authority, as would professional journals such as NEJM.

The same holds true if your paper is taking the opposite stance, that naturopathic remedies are better than pharmaceutical ones. If the site you plan to quote is operated by the distributor of vitamins or natural foods, there's a good chance your information will be questionable, too.

When it comes to using online sources, always be wary of dot-com tags (except for reputable newspapers and magazines). Instead, rely on tags with *org, edu,* and *gov.*

And when it comes to incorporating hard copy texts, periodicals and professional journals are seen as more reliable than popular magazines. For example, journals published by the American Psychological Association are considered more authoritative than articles appearing in Psychology Today. That's not a dig at Psychology today, which is a respected magazine. The difference is this: popular magazine articles are chosen by editors to suit their editorial needs. Professional journal pieces, such as the APA journals, however, are subject to peer review by other professionals. They determine whether or not the pieces are suitable to publish on the basis of whether or not they break new ground.

The best way to begin your research is to familiarize yourself with the college or university library. Make an appointment with a librarian who can lead you through the maze of computer resources. The electronic book catalog (forget my days of thumbing through drawers of cards) is a great way to start. Even if a library doesn't have the text you want, many college and universities offer an inter-library exchange that let you reserve the book and have it shipped to your librarian's doorstep.

Also, ask your school's librarian to show you how to access electronic databases for periodicals (*EbscoHost* and *Aacdemic Universe* to name a couple) and journals, biographies, government journals, newspapers, essays, pamphlets, even audio-visual and film resources. The librarians are there to serve you, and my observation has been that they are more than eager to help because too few students take advantage of this valuable resource.

So now you are on your way. You have entered the world of research. You will scroll though bibliographies, abstracts, and eventually the books and articles you will use.

As you gather printouts and photocopies, it's important that you organize your work properly. I always recommend an accordion folder. If you begin organizing your work physically, it will make it that much easier when you sit down to write. Keep a yellow marker handy as you read each piece, highlighting the information you plan to use. Write notes in the margins or jot down points on index cards. You may want to write a summary, called a précis, of each article. And always, always, always make sure you can account where you got each bit of information you plan to use.

And that brings us to the other caveat—always giving credit where credit is due. In an age of cut and paste and easy access to secondary sources—not to mention an age in which research papers can be bought online—plagiarism is a serious concern, one that could reach epidemic proportions if it were not for schools today demanding in-text citations.

What is plagiarism? It's the unethical—and illegal use of someone else's work and passing it off as your own. It's the theft of another's intellectual property. And when it comes to theft, an intellectual property is no different from a tangible one. Plagiarism, if you're caught, can also sound your academic death knell. Professors, armed with TurnItIn.com and other web-based plagiarism assessment services to seek out cheats, will be left with no other choice than to fail you.

So, it *is* a big deal for you to learn how to properly credit the sources you use. It's a question of ethics, the *ethos* part that supports the triangle *logos* and *pathos* necessary for good writing.

Naturally, anyone who tries to lift another's work and pass it off as his or her own elicits little sympathy once the ax falls. But what about the person who unintentionally plagiarizes, the student who is so intent on impressing readers that he or she neglects to cite important passages? Unfortunately, it's still plagiarism. It's still using someone else's work without acknowledgment.

"But it's not plagiarism," some students insist, 'if I just take some of the ideas I read and reword them, using my own words and style, right?"

Wrong! You could be guilty of paraphrased plagiarism, especially if you're borrowing information about a subject in which you're no expert. "Hmm,," a professor might muse, "so you really know first-hand about UN inspectors. Or performing open heart surgery?"

Ergo, it's important you cover yourself with proper in-text citations and a "Works Cited" page, the old bibliography, at the end of your paper. Even if you don't cite from some of the materials you've read, it's also a good idea to list the works you have consulted under a separate heading, "Works Consulted."

Where do you start? Most English courses require that you use either the Modern Language Association (MLA) or American Psychological Association (APA) formats for citing. MLA is the format of choice in the English departments I have taught, though some allow science and nursing majors, for example to use APA.

At first blush, MLA style, citing, and listing can seem daunting. But the task is a relatively easy once you get the hang of it. Citing, for the most part, in involves parenthetical citations at the end of the lines you use. And don't feel you have to commit each comma, period, parenthesis, indent, etc. to memory. There are a number of handbooks and websites out there to help you.

For both APA and MLA formatting and style, a popular website is The Purdue University Online Writing Lab at http://owl.english.purdue.edu. It's titled "The Owl At Purdue: Free Writing Help and Teaching Resources Open 24/7," and it serves writers from around the world.

For APA, another valuable site is www.ccc.commnet.edu/apa. Prepared by the Humanities department at Hartford, Connecticut's Capital Community College and the Arthur C. Banks, Jr. Library, the online "A Guide for Writing Research Papers based on Styles Recommended by the American Psychological Association" is a soup to nuts site that with questions and answers on everything from manuscript formatting to headings to incorporating graphics and tables to quotations to last-minute corrections. If you must use APA, you must visit this site.

When it comes to writing handbooks that include MLA and APA there are a slew of them. You'll find them in the college bookstore, usually offered as adjuncts to the main, encyclopedic writing texts.

But for my money, and as someone who reveres primary sources, why not go to the primary sources—the APA and the MLA? Both have their own Web-sites *www.apa.org* and *www.mla.org* plus their own handbooks: *Publication Manual of the American Psychological Association* and *MLA Handbook for Writers of Research Papers.* My MLA bias, of course, leads me to favor the latter. Written by Joseph Gibaldi, MLA Handbook is now in its sixth edition.

Sometimes, the best way to study proper in-text citations is to review polished papers to see how it is done. With that said, I'd like to share with you some MLA formatted freshman composition research papers I received in the Fall of 2007 at Norwalk Community College.

HEALTHCARE FOR ALL

By C. Emma Villavicencio

At twenty years of age I had an accident while quickly descending the stairs in my home. In my haste, I missed the last three or four steps and landed heavily on the side of my foot. I did not know the extent of my injuries but I felt tremendous pain and was unable to stand, so an ambulance was called to take me to the hospital. After a doctor's examination I discovered that I had badly sprained my ankle and chipped a bone in my leg. This injury would require a hard cast to keep my ankle immobilized and protected for six weeks. As a whole this unfortunate accident resulted in: an ambulance ride, an emergency room visit, a doctors consult, an orthopedic cast fitting, crutches, and follow up visits to ensure the proper healing of my ankle. The total cost to me for all of these procedures was zero dollars, or should I say pounds. Fortunately for me, I was living in England when this accident occurred. England has a national healthcare system that provides free medical services to all its citizens. Had the same thing occurred a few years later when I was living and working in New York, the financial repercussions to my limited budget would have been devastating! At that time I was in a similar position as the 47 million Americans, which includes nine million children, who currently do not have health insurance in the United States ("The Uninsured"). It is past time that the United States joins the rest of the industrialized countries that have already decided to provide their people with health care. Healthcare reform is necessary in this country in the form of a single payer system.

A national health care system would provide a number of benefits. The most important benefit would be providing all Americans with healthcare, a seemingly basic right, regardless of age, race, or economic status. The cost of utilizing a single payer plan would be comparable to or possibly less than the current healthcare spending. Also, it would decrease bureaucracy by eliminating many layers of insurance paperwork patients and doctors are forced to go through in our current system, which in turn would reduce costs. Another benefit would be an increase in life expectancy by allowing more financially conscious Americans to receive adequate prevention and early care instead of waiting until an illness becomes worse. All of these reasons point towards a national health care program as the solution the United States requires. There are opponents of single payer systems, mostly financed by insurance companies that stand to lose billions from such a plan. These opponents point to some of the other countries that have enacted such plans as an advisory against our following suit. However, those that oppose fail to take into account some of the methods unique to these particular countries and overstate some of the problems, while understating and ignoring America's own.

A single payer plan basically means that doctors, hospitals, and other care providers would be paid through one agency instead of the many different payers that make up our current fragmented system. Cost is often cited as a major reason that a universal healthcare plan would not be widely accepted. It is understandable to assume that providing coverage for everyone would be more expensive than current costs. However, many state studies show that the reworking of the system to a single payer not-for-profit plan would cost the same or even less than we are paying today ("How Much"). There are a number of reasons why a reformed plan would save money. Cutting the costs of administration by using a single agency would save billions of dollars each year. Buying medical equipment and drugs in bulk would provide even more savings. There most likely would be a minimal 'health tax' levied on citizens but current policy holders would no longer have premiums or co-payments and would therefore be paying less. The Healthcare for All Californians Act states that its reformed program would cover "medically appropriate hospital inpatient and outpatient care, emergency room visits, physician services (including preventive care), prescription drugs, lab tests, mental health and substance abuse treatment, eyeglasses and other services. The program would also cover home health and adult daycare services for the aged and/or disabled. Dental care would be covered along with vision exams and hearing" (Sheils). This is much more coverage than many policyholders currently possess. Why would we not switch to a plan that provides comprehensive medical care to all when it costs no more?

Another benefit of having a national health plan is that it would decrease the amount of bureaucracy in the system which is now plagued with red tape and inefficiency. Most people can relate with the frustration that comes along with getting an insurance company to approve the physician or procedure required. A new plan would allow people to visit a doctor, even if away from home, without first having to call their insurance company to find one that is approved. Also, patients would not have to petition their insurance company to get approval to see a specialist that was recommended by their general practitioner. Having a national health system would give patients a broader array of choices in selecting a doctor they are comfortable with. People would be able to choose the physician they want rather than the one their insurance company thinks will cost them the least amount of money. A national single payer system would allow cohesiveness throughout the country reducing competition between practices. Doctors would no longer have to compete for business and would be able to direct their energies towards caring for their patients. An article in the *New England Journal of Medicine* states that 31% of healthcare expenditures in the U.S. are administrative costs, while countries with a single payer system, such as Canada spend only 16.7% (Woolhandler). A reformed plan would save medical practices and hospitals large sums of money and stress by reducing their paperwork load. Doctors would no longer have pressures from insurance and drug companies therefore allowing their focus to be on their patients' best interests.

The adaptation of a single payer health care system would provide better care for those who already have insurance as well as those who lack it. Many HMO's and insurance companies place stringent limits on the types of medical procedures that can be obtained by those it covers. Sometimes even standard exams and procedures are denied by companies whose first priority is to the profit line. A universal health care program would allow for a wide standardization of coverage so that everyone could be eligible for necessary procedures, and not just those select few who happen to have the right health care plan. As a result of the current health system, the United States has fallen well behind most of the OECD (Organization for Economic Co-operation and Development) in life expectancy. While most OECD countries have experienced large gains in life expectancy over the past 40 years, the increase of 7.3 years in the U.S. is well below that of Japan 14 years, Canada 8.4 years, and below the OECD average as a whole. To compound the problem the United States spent 15% of its GDP (Gross Domestic Product) on health care in 2003, which is not only the highest percentage of all the countries that are part of the OECD but also almost double the average of 8.6% spent by other countries (Chua). The inefficiency and ineffectiveness of the current system is as glaring as it is costly.

One major reason for our poor statistics in regards to the rest of the world is that with restrictive costs placed on health care, people are more likely to put off getting the medical attention needed until they absolutely have to. Illnesses and injuries are easiest to treat when they are in their earlier stages and have not done major damage to the body yet. People with no insurance or inadequate medical insurance are more likely to avoid seeing a doctor until the problem becomes too painful to bear. If people were to have their problems treated earlier, before they progress and become more serious, their chances for a successful recovery would increase drastically. This would also aid in keeping costs down as it is usually cheaper to treat an illness in the early stages rather than in the later ones. Expectant mothers are also less likely to receive proper prenatal care in this country, resulting in our higher infant mortality rate. In 2002, the infant mortality rate in the U.S. was 7 deaths per 1,000 live births, above the OECD average of 6.1. Other OECD countries such as Japan, Iceland, Sweden, Finland, and Norway all have infant mortality rates below 3.5, half that of the U.S. (Chua).

The idea of moving to a national health care system is not without opposition. The Heritage Foundation, one of the detractors of a national health care program points to the experiences of countries such as Great Britain and Canada as being less than successful. Robert Kuttner of the Boston Globe points out that in the case of Great Britain these problems arise not from the health care system itself, but rather from the small amount of money that is put into it. By investing only 6% of its GDP into the health care system Britain cannot expect to provide adequately for its citizens. Meanwhile even though the U.S. spends 15% of its GDP on healthcare, the life expectancy in the U.S. is 75 years, three less than that of Britain which has a life expectancy of 78. Other countries with national health systems that spend 9 or 10 percent of their GDP have life expectancies over 80 years. Kuttner adds that if the U.S. adopted a universal plan, it could decrease the amount spent on healthcare to 10% of its GDP, and still greatly improve the system and provide better results than Britain. Likewise, some people question the ability of Canada's current system to deliver treatments in a timely manner and advocate adopting a private system like the one in the United States. However, supporters of the current system recognize that switching to a private model would cause inequalities with only the wealthy being able to afford certain treatments. As it is, Canada's current system has one of the highest life expectancies (80 years) and lowest infant mortality rate of industrialized countries, which can be attributed to their health care system ("Canadian Health"). In addition, Canada is burdened by its close proximity to the United States.

Uninsured Americans have been known to cross into Canada to receive free medical care.

One of the biggest problems that face the American people is our dysfunctional healthcare system. Arnold Relman states in his book *A Second Opinion* that "Healthcare expenditures are currently rising at an average annual rate of over 7% which is more than twice the rate of inflation" (44). He estimates that by 2015, the U.S. will be spending over $4 trillion on healthcare, which will be approximately 20% of the GDP. This spending is ludicrous considering that 18,000 people die annually from a lack of medical insurance ("Single-Payer"). Personally, I have experienced healthcare in a country which has a national health system, as well as living in the U.S. both with and without health insurance. Growing up in England, I took for granted that a doctor would see me no matter how insignificant my malady, without ever a concern about cost. Living in the U.S without any health coverage made me fully appreciate my previous situation. After moving to this country, I discovered that getting sick was no longer an option. That basic right of having free or at least affordable healthcare was gone. I currently am fortunate enough to have insurance coverage and can only hope there comes a day in the near future when every person living in America can have that same peace of mind.

Works Cited and Consulted

"Canadian Health Care Introduction." Canadian Health Care. 3 Nov. 2007 <http://www.canadian-healthcare.org/index.html>.

Chua, Kao-Ping. "The Case for Universal Healthcare." American Medical Student Association. 2006. 3 Nov. 2007 <http://www.amsa.org/uhc/CaseForUHC.pdf>.

"How Much Would A Single Payer System Cost?" Physicians for a National Health Program. Feb 2005. 3 Nov. 2007 <http://www.pnhp.org/facts>.

Kuttner, Robert. "The Efficiency of Universal Healthcare." Boston Globe. 12 Feb. 2000. 3 Nov. 2007 <http://www.commondreams.org/views/021300-101.htm>.

Relman, Arnold S. A Second Opinion: Rescuing America's Health Care. New York: PublicAffairs, 2007.

Sered, Susan Starr and Rushika Fernandopulle. Uninsured in America: Life and Death in the Land of Opportunity. California: University of California Press, 2007.

Sheils, John F. and Randall A. Haught. "The Health Care for All Californians

Act: Cost and Economic Impacts Analysis." Health Care for All – California. 19 Jan. 2005. 3 Nov. 2007 <http://www.healthcareforall.org/summary.pdf>.

"Single-Payer FAQ" Physicians for a National Health Program. 2006. 3 Nov. 2007 <http://pnhp.org/facts/singlepayer_faq.php>.

"The Uninsured: A Primer" Kaiser Family Foundation. Oct 2007. 3 Nov. 2007 <http://www.kff.org/uninsured/upload/7451-03.pdf>.

Woolhandler, Steffie, Terry Campbell and David U. Himmelstein. "Costs of Health Care Administration in the United States and Canada" New England Journal of Medicine. 21 Aug. 2003. 3 Nov. 2007 <http://content.nejm.org>.

DOCTORS PRESCRIBING FOR PAYROLL

By Marina Kovalskiy

There seems to be a growing number of physicians prescribing unnecessary medication to patients. The main reason behind this is the benefits that pharmaceutical companies provide to the doctors. Sales representatives offer big-screen TVs, computers, fax machines, and paid golf vacations if the doctors prescribe their new drugs. Do consumers really need these medications or is it driven by profit?

The drug companies are corrupting the doctors by offering money and other benefits. As a result, the patient cannot rely on doctors to be totally objective and truthful about their health. It is therefore dangerous to conclude that traditional medicine is the best way to go. We have to be knowledgeable ourselves since the doctors mostly go by what drug companies say. If a doctor is thinking about all his expenses to be paid it could affect which drug is administered to the patient. Take a look at two recent examples. Vioxx was heavily promoted as a new pain killer and widely prescribed. The successful Hormone Replacement Therapy (HRT), convinced physicians that HRT prevented cardiovascular disease before even one single clinical trial had been done to confirm this. In other words, HRT was promoted and physicians prescribed it without any evidence to show that HRT prevented cardiovascular disease. Major tragedies followed. "There were estimated 88,000-140,000 excess cases of serious coronary artery disease attributable to Vioxx in the United States alone" (haiap.org).

As a result the number of women harmed by severe adverse effect of HRT, which include breast cancer, may have been even larger because HRT was used for a longer time. When the tragedy unfolded and the media reported it, both Vioxx and HRT were withdrawn by the manufacturers. Dr. David Graham, a research scientist who works for the FDA, is the one who found the problems with Vioxx, the pain-killing drug. Dr. Graham told a senate investigating committee that his research indicated that Vioxx caused up tremendous amount of hearth attacks and strokes. The FDA, which seems to be an employee of Big-Pharma-Government, tried to intimidate Dr. Graham and other reviewers when they pointed out the safety concerns that Vioxx might do more than kill the pain. It was killing patients." Hughes Hubbard & Reed spokesman Kent Jarrell recognizes that Merck has its hands full in defending its first Vioxx case: "Mark Lanier is a good, flamboyant attorney," says Jarrell, and the suit is being tried in a county that is historically friendly to plaintiffs. Jarrell contends, however, that the trial will be no cakewalk for the plaintiffs either "This is not a nor-mal Vioxx case, which is about the risk of heart attacks and strokes being increased by the use of the drug," Jarrell says. "Lanier is going to make this about the behavior of the company. We plan on making it about the specifics of causation" (law).

Continued research on this topic turned up many articles, but one of them really touched my heart very deeply. Mary Linnen, 29, decided to lose some weight before her wedding. Her doctor prescribed her a drug known as Fen-Phen. After 23 days of taking this medication Mary experienced a dizziness and shortness of breath. After that, her doc-tor told her to stop using this drug and did not examine her. Her symp-toms got worse, treating her health to the point that she collapsed at work. Six month later she was rushed to the emergency room and diag-nosed with primary pulmonary hypertension: the capillaries that sent oxygen to her lungs had thickened and were closing, suffocating her. She died three months later in the arms of her fiancé.

> A new drug billed as a magic bullet for obesity called Rimonabant, which helps people lose weight, although not that much weight. It also helps lower cardiac risk factors, according to a review of studies. The Rimonabant studies took place in 350 trial centers in the United States, Canada and Europe. The 6,625 participants were at least 18 years old, which were overweight, or obese. One study focused solely on people being treated for diabetes and another group of people with high cholesterol, or high blood pres-sure. The authors described the weight loss pattern: "After the 36th week, the level of weight loss decreased and the body weight was maintained practically until the end of the

studies." One study evaluated data after two years: "Patients who stayed on 20 mg Rimonabant seemed to maintain their weight loss, while those who were re-randomized gained significant weight." People on the larger dose lost an average 1.5 inches on their waistlines. They also showed a slight dip in blood pressure. The higher drug dose significantly lowered blood lipids (fats) and increased high-density lipoprotein ("good" cholesterol) by 3.5 mg/dl compared to placebo. On the flip side, side effects included nausea, dizziness, headache, joint pain and diarrhea. More serious side effects included psychiatric and nervous system disorders.

We, as consumers, should be more educated and knowledgeable about what is good for us and what is not. The theory of "one size fits all" will not apply to the subject related of our health. Award-winning investigative reporter Alicia Mundy provides shocking news about the whole debacle. "The Battle over Fen-Phen tells the story of the legal battle against the pharmaceutical companies after Fen-Phen's users started dying-some, like Linnen, of primary pulmonary hypertension; others of heart valve damage. Investigative reporter Alicia Mundy weaves a dramatic tale from the development of the drugs to FDA approval to the final litigation. Pharmaceutical companies know about the risks and side affects of these medications plenty, according to the evidence Mundy reveals" (newstarget).

Is the drug industry fully responsible for all of this? Some people will say yes and others will say no. Doctors should be primarily responsible for the health of their patients. The British House of Commons Health Committee 2005, in its report stated: "It is quite wrong to look upon the drug industry as the corrupters and doctors as the corrupted. Doctors should share equal responsibility for the debased relationship." (newstarget)". The committee also said that regulatory authorities are close to this industry and won't ensure that it works in the public interests. To do the things right way doctors should stop taking free gifts, grants and pharmaceutical samples. This will prevent meetings with doctors and sales representatives. The decision making of prescribing drugs should be based on scientific evidences such as blood work tests, diagnostic images and not on the gifts and other rewards. The distribution of the pharmaceutical samples should be prohibited by law. It might be replaced with the coupons or vouchers for low-income families. The availability and excess of these free samples increase stimulus for physicians and patients to rely on these medications, which are definitely expensive, but not effective. For instance, many patients with high blood pressure of diabetes can be easily treated with regular, well-established medications, which are less expensive. Unfortunately some patients already started their treatment with these new and highly priced drugs.

Pharmaceutical companies make people sick and at the same time are creating more business for hospitals. People should not die from weight loss or pain killer pills.

So we, as citizens, should make a stand to stop this crime that is harming our children and our loved ones. We need to spread the word as fast as possible. Physicians prescribing unnecessary medication to patients should immediately stop this action. We need to be more aware about the care we receive. Doctors should continue to practice the real medicine, based on their knowledge and experience.

Work Cited

Adams, Mark. "Experiment shows medical doctors to be glorified drug dealers, easily manipulated by drug companies." Newstarget on the Web 7 Jul. 2005. 29 Oct. 2007 <http://www.newstarget.com/2005/07/07>.

Balasubramaniam, Phil. "Unethical Drug Promotion and Public Health." Haiap on the Web 15 Sept. 2003. 22 Oct. 2007 <http://haiap.org /2003/09/15/unethical>.

Donald, Mark. "Lawyers in First Vioxx Suit Battle Over Causation." Law on the Web 15 Jul. 2007. 12 Oct 2007 <http://www.law.com/jsp/article>.

"Merck Voluntarily Recalls Vioxx® After Experts Claim it Can Cause Serious Injury." 21 Oct. 2007 <http://www.fenphennews.com/hl/x_vioxx>.

Getting There: From Idea to Polished Prose

Sitting Down to Write

Okay, you have an idea, a thesis, a point you want to drive home to a larger audience. How does it all happen? How does it go from head to paper like those argumentative/research essays you read in the last chapter?

I know, it's easier said than done, but the point is it can be done if you take some logical steps guided by your passion for the idea.

"Huh?" you ask. I'm talking about steps, a roadmap. Rarely can writers craft great essays off the top of their head, and it's a fair assumption that beginning writers never will. Good writing takes work. It involves having an idea, having enough information to support it, organizing your thoughts in a coherent manner, writing your first draft, editing it, writing a second version, revising and editing it again, and at the very least, a third, polished draft on which you will feel comfortable adding your name.

Ouch! Sound like a lot of work, right? Yes, but if you are going to master anything in life, it is going to take effort. Eventually it will become easier, but it will never be easy. Not if it's to be good.

Before you begin to cringe, let me begin with Step #1: Relax.

"What?" you ask. "You just told me it's not going to be easy. How can I relax?"

I'm not saying that you have a drink, put your feet up and take a nap. What I'm saying is don't panic. For complex tasks you'll need life's greatest tool, your brain, to minimize any anxiety. Sure, anxiety has its place in busy work, emergency efforts and assembly line tasks, but great thoughts typically don't flow from heads clouded with fear.

So, make yourself comfortable, but not too comfortable. Find a place that's physically and psychologically amenable to your thought processes. If you think better in quiet settings, seek them out. If you're the type who needs background noise or music playing for comfort, let the music play.

Once you've collected and physically spread out the information to support your point, dare to write, whether it's pen or pencil to paper or fingers to the keyboard–which ever makes you feel more comfortable. (It's interesting to note that in the days before typewriters, writing seemed to have a more natural, less digital flow from hand to pen to paper. In poring over old magazines, the writing appeared to be more thoughtful, or, dare I say because it seems like such clichéd blather, organic.)

Whatever medium you choose, you will start out staring at empty space, a vast void, which can be quite scary. You might feel your heart beating faster than the cursor flashes.

Now for the leap. Some people will recommend freewriting, just putting down whatever comes into your head as a way to break the ice, sort of a literary sketching exercise. While this approach can get you started, it also leaves you with a lot of random thoughts, a screen litter of superfluous tangents you will have to wade through to find relevant passages.

Others might suggest a rough outline of all the points you want to make to support your thesis. At least this approach gives you a physical framework within which to work. As mentioned earlier, your outline will be either chronological or spatial, from one step to the next, or from one room to another, as if you were a real estate agent showing off a house to support your main thesis, which is why the prospective buyer should purchase it.

Some pedagogues, a.k.a. teachers, require a detailed outline, one you'll tack on at the beginning of your paper. While this is great for a master's or doctoral thesis, I see it as busywork for a freshman composition course, one that impedes the creative process, hamstringing students to following a rigid outline whether they want to or not. I've found some papers like this to have as much heart as technical manuals, which isn't much.

So how do you start? Some people just throw ideas onto the screen and seeing what sticks. Some texts talk about clustering, compartmentalizing ideas like planets in the solar system. Not my style.

The point is, there really is no set way to begin writing, just as there is not set way of viewing the world. How you begin to craft your prose is all a matter of individual preference. The important point is that you begin. You sit down to write in an area that will be conducive to your creative process, and that you take that first step.

Sketching it Out

Remember the chapter on introductions? Okay, you know what a good intro requires and that it should state your thesis. And you know that a good thesis should be able to stand on its own, be a complete thought, not fragmented, and never ever a question.

Let's say, for example, the thesis you've come up with for your environmentally-sensitive paper is, "The production and widespread use of bio-fuels will not only lessen America's dependency on foreign oil, but it will dramatically cut greenhouse gasses while fueling new industries and our nation's overall economy."

It reads like a pretty solid thesis statement, one you can cut out, paste on the wall and everybody who reads it will know your paper in a nutshell.

Now, for the whole nut. What information from your research, theoretically speaking, of course, will you use, and how will you organize it?

From a very simplistic point of view, we know that essays are composed of paragraphs, and each paragraph has a main point called its topic sentence. The topic sentence is the heart of the paragraph, a mini-thesis. It can appear anywhere in the paragraph from the first line to somewhere in the middle to the last line. But regardless of where it goes, if must be there.

Let's see, perhaps in your first paragraph, your topic sentence that our nation has to reduce its dependency on foreign oil because most of it is imported from unstable parts of the globe, putting our nation's security at risk.

Your next paragraph's main point is that unlike foreign oil, bio-fuels can be produced within our own borders from corn, woodchips and switch grass.

The third paragraph, describes how bio-fuels are much cleaner than fossil fuels, lessening the amount of greenhouse gasses contributing to global warming.

Your fourth paragraph explains how such new, homegrown industries can bolster the American economy and even open the door to boosting alternative, adjunct industries such as wind and solar power.

The fifth paragraph, gleaned, of course from your extensive research, might describe how some states have already set timetables for cutting their oil dependency by 30 percent by the year 2020. The same paragraph might also tell how different states are working with industry to cut greenhouse gasses, winning their cooperation to embrace alternative fuels.

By now you see how each topic sentence of each paragraph serves to support your thesis. Perhaps you will come up with a half-dozen to a dozen topics that will shore-up your thesis. The more supporting paragraphs you have, the better. You will make a much stronger case.

As you move from paragraph to paragraph, you will want to make sure they follow a logical sequence. Transitional words, at stated earlier, will also make the reader's ride a little smoother. Prepositional phrases such as, "On the other hand," "At the same time," "In addition to," "Beyond that," serve as visual road signs facilitating the reader's journey. Remember, you want to leave the reader thinking, not dizzy, or with a bad case of whiplash. Read and reread how your paragraphs connect to make sure your essay flows. Also note that transitional phrases alone will not give your essay the right flow. Logic will.

Breathing Life into Your Prose through Quotes

As you write your essay, never underestimate the power of quotes, not just the ones you are going to cite from other published sources, but ones from live people. Why quotes? Because they breathe life into any piece of writing. Quotes make characters jump off the page—in their own words, not yours. We get to hear each character's cadence, tone, his or her voice.

If it's a heady research paper you're putting together, an important person's voice will lend a new sense of authority. If the essay you're writing is a human interest piece, whether it's from observation or memory, quotes will add to the human dimension.

When you search your notes for the best quotes, don't choose ones that merely convey information. That's the lazy writer's way out, quoting someone rattling off a paragraph of facts when you should paraphrase them, giving credit where credit is due through in-text citations or attribution. Look for quotes that have an emotional component, one that underscores the information while adding a certain dramatic quality.

For example, let's return to that bio-fuel essay we were describing. You interview or quote a famous environmentalist, Prof. I Knowitall, who says: "Our statistics show that appropriate measures taken today to employ bio-fuel technologies via corn, wood chips and switch grass in our Southern and Mid-Western states, plus cooperation from major oil companies who will back research and development, will prove beneficial in decades to come as projections point to a 20 percent reduction in the carbon footprint over the continental United States by the year 2065. Homegrown, healthy for the environment and a money-maker to boot. Without a doubt, I've seen the future of energy in this country, and that future is bio-fuel."

Wow! There's a lot of information in that quote, a lot to sort out. The lazy writer will just drop it all in as if his or her writing talents – not to mention critical thinking – were not much more than a tape recorder.

I ask you, what part of it jumps out? What part seems the most human? It's this quote: "Homegrown, healthy for the environment and a moneymaker to boot. Without a doubt, I've seen the future of energy in this country, and that future is bio-fuel."

What about the other information? Of course you should use it, *you* being the operative word. Paraphrase the rest of the quote to give the reader important facts. After all, this is not just a sound-byte paper. But . . . it shouldn't be a dry, textbook one either. So, you need to develop an ear for quotes.

Quotes are a wonderful thing. They make literature sing, essays more human and lend credibility to opinion pieces. Again, they breathe life into writing. So as you prepare your research, underline or highlight not just the information you are going to use and cite. Note the quotes you will use to make your writing pop right off the page.

In Conclusion? Don't You Dare

Those two words, "In conclusion," make many writing teachers – and readers—roll their eyes. You might as well just stamp amateur on your paper. "But I *am* an amateur writer," you fire back.

No, you're a beginning writer who must cast off all amateurish ways.

So, how do you wrap up this essay you've poured your head and heart into, not to mention hours of research and planning? There is no set formula, but after you have covered all of the points to support your thesis, it will be time to wrap it up. However, do not end in an abrupt, halting way, a la Loony Tunes' "That's all folks."

It has to be a thoughtful ending, and thought provoking, too.

Most rhetoricians and writing professors suggest you end by restating your thesis. While that's essentially true, don't take that suggestion too literally. Restate your main point in a different manner. The last thing you want your *last thing* to look like is a verbatim copy and paste job. That's as formulaic, if not as obnoxious as "In conclusion," and it can create the impression of repetition.

Remember the bio-fuel example? This was the thesis: "The production and widespread use of bio-fuels will not only lessen America's dependency on foreign oil, but it will dramatically cut greenhouse gasses while fueling new industries and our nation's overall economy."

Here's a poor, lazy person's ending, "In conclusion, the production and widespread use of bio-fuels will not only lessen America's dependency on foreign oil, but it will dramatically cut greenhouse gasses while fueling new industries and our nation's overall economy."

It's a snooze, and it shows that you didn't think enough about your topic to come up with a clever ending, so why should I, the reader, give a hoot.

Say it differently. Tie your essay together with a quote, an example, an anecdote, or a scene setter to leave the reader thinking. Restate your thesis through the eyes or words of an individual who epitomizes your main point. End with a "what might happen" proposition if your point is or isn't heeded. Do anything but what you just read in the above "in conclusion" example.

Wouldn't something like this be a lot better?

"Dr. Knowitall says that he used to stare out at Los Angeles sunsets, pretty as they are, with a sense of dread about the environment left to his grandchildren. But now, with the resurgence of bio-fuel interests and government incentives for companies to embrace alternative energy, Dr. Knowitall sees a silver lining beyond the smoggy skies.

"There's hope for a better tomorrow, a realistic hope, now that alternative energy is finally being demanded by our culture," he said. "We have to keep the momentum going if America and the planet are going to survive."

This type of conclusion not only restates the main point, leaving the reader thinking. It's also a call for action. In many ways it is even more powerful that the thesis.

That's how you should handle conclusions, without selling yourself—or the readers—short.

Making it Worthy of Your Name

There's the old line that in real estate the three most things are "Location, location, location." In freshman composition it can be said that the three most important words are "Revision, revision, revision." Rule # 7,

"The Secret of Writing is in the Rewriting," states this quite clearly. But getting there takes work, and the last thing many beginning writers want to do after sweating through a first draft is to face it again—and again. But you must if your paper is going to be your best possible effort, worthy enough to display your name as author. "The quality goes in before the name goes on," was the old advertising slogan for Zenith color televisions. It's a slogan that writers should live by, too.

So, don't become aggravated by revisions. Think of them as opportunities to make your work better. Think of them as second, third, even fourth chances. Where else in life do you get a chance for a "do over?" Maybe you find it in the movie "Groundhog Day," where the main character gets a chance to relive each day over and over again until he gets it right. But in the real world, one rarely gets a second chance to set things straight. How many other courses give you that opportunity?

In writing classes, it's all part of the process because your first draft *is* a work in progress. And this class is about that process. We revise. All writers do.

The methods I prefer my students to follow involves peer review and peer editing. Peer review is valuable because students get to read their papers aloud in class. (I know the shy and reticent among you are swearing right now.) This way your classmates and your professor can offer input about what they liked and what could be improved. This kind of review goes to the heart of your essay, showing how it is perceived by your audience.

Peer editing is the other approach, and I must confess that when I first started teaching, I had my doubts about this established method. I cynically thought peer editing was the lazy professor's way out, an invention thought up by a teacher who needed time out to do his taxes during class. I questioned its effectiveness despite the English Department touting it as a way to make students better writers by being editors, too.

The first couple of times it proved to be the blind leading the blind, if not the blind confusing the sighted. Just think about it. There's one student who has mastered English and has nearly perfect prose. And someone with no grammar savvy is about to "improve" it! This so-called student "editor" inserts double negatives, wrong subject-verb agreement (She works. No, "She work."), and puts in commas with the reckless abandon of someone sprinkling grass seed.

Peer editing only works with ground rules. First, have your grammar handbook, dictionary, and thesaurus at the ready. Second, you don't have to accept everything your peer editor suggests, which brings us back to the first ground rule. Challenge their corrections by the book.

Most importantly, I ask students to be a reader first, an editor second.

"Think about what you just read," I recall telling my first composition class. "What's the point, the thesis? How does it flow?"

"Remember, people are putting themselves on the line here. They're exposing part of themselves."

A few students snickered.

"I mean it. It takes guts to write some of these essays. Treat them with respect."

And respect they did, sometimes too much so.

"I think it's real good," was common rejoinder, only to find inarticulate ramblings that were barely corrected aside for an errant period.

"Don't be too nice," I followed up. "You're not helping the person at all if you keep telling them it's great when it's not. Remember that saying, you've got to be cruel to be kind sometimes. We're here to give constructive criticism. Give them the good and the bad. Be sensitive, but not too sensitive."

Here are the parameters that make peer editing work. Read it as a reader first, and then as an editor, one who evaluates myriad items. Rate the title. Is it good? Can you come up with a better one? What about the introduction? Is the thesis clearly stated, or is it implied? What about the organization? Do the paragraphs flow smoothly with good transitions? How does the writer incorporate quotes and cite secondary sources? What about the conclusion?

These are important evaluations before you take your pen to the hard copy and begin to search for common grammatical errors. What are they? The serious ones English professors look for are: fragments, run-on sentences, improper subject/verb agreement, wrong tenses, and punctuation problems.

Any good college handbook can help save you from these grammatical pitfalls. Two good ones are *The Bedford Handbook* and Strunk and White's *Elements of Style*. By all means, buy one and keep it throughout your college career and beyond. (Hang on to this book, too.) While this text is not designed as a grammar primer, here's some sound grammatical advice.

1.) Watch Out for Fragments.

A fragment is an incomplete thought. That is, it's a line without a subject and a verb. Is this a grave, grammatical sin? Not always. Professional writers use them often for emphasis, cadence, and to build a rhythm. In fact, I just used one with "Not always." Where's the subject? Where's the verb? It's a fragment. I admit it. Guilty as charged. Ooops! Another fragment. Many composition teachers will steer you away from such literary underscoring because they want to train you to always incorporate a subject and a predicate, a verb, in your sentences. But more and more professors, upon seeing fragments used in a proper, professional sense, appreciate them.

Actually, they are not the fragments that trigger the strict grammarian's alarm system. The fragments that cause concern are those where it is obvious that the writer didn't know he or she had an incomplete thought. For example, look at the following line: "Walking down the avenue this past Monday with Peter and Marie." The grammatically challenged will argue that walking is a verb (It's actually a gerund here.) and that Peter and Marie must be the subjects. They are not. This so-called sentence leaves the reader hanging, wanting to know what happened.

When asked to fix it, this same student might write, "Walking down the avenue this past Monday with Peter and Marie in the neighborhood where I was born." It's still not complete. That entire clause can not stand on its own. However, if you changed it to, "Walking down the avenue this past Monday with Peter and Marie in the neighborhood I was born, I became sentimental," you would have a complete thought. The independent clause here is, "I became sentimental." The dependent clause is the first part, and it's called dependent because it can not stand alone.

If you have two independent clauses, each one can stand alone, and you have a compound sentence. Here's one: "Peter and Marie walked with me into my old neighborhood yesterday, and I because sentimental." Here you have two independent clauses, and they must be separated by a comma and a conjunction, which is this case is "and." And that leads us to the next writing hurdle new writers must jump, run-on sentences.

2.) Steer Clear of Run-on Sentences.

Unlike fragments that are incomplete thoughts, run-on sentences are indiscrete thoughts. They are not separated. They just flow from one to the other without any breaks. The writer seems to be speaking in random variation, what we used to call scatterbrained. Here is an example: "We were driving through Provence last summer there was a small farmhouse that Marge spotted from the road since she read French Marge told me they had rooms to let we decided to stay we stayed for a week."

I know this sounds like an exaggeration, an extreme example I dug up to make a point about run-ons, but many a writing instructor, I'm sorry to say, has come across similar examples. The writer doesn't know when to catch a breath. Perhaps these writers feel that stopping will close the thought valve. Who knows? Maybe instant messaging and text messaging are to blame. That mindset values speed of communication over grammatical and punctuation propriety. It seems to regard the rules of Standard English as unimportant. These people don't even capitalize, for crying out loud.

Let's edit the run-on sentence above. You can break it down into four sentences. "We were driving through Provence last summer. There was a small farmhouse that Marge spotted setback from the road. Since she read French, Marge told me they had rooms to let. We decided to stay we stayed for a week."

By doing so, you avoid a long-winded, run-on sentence, and it is grammatically correct. Still, the writing still seems choppy. Let's smooth it out a bit. Transform the first two short sentences into a compound one. "We were driving through Provence last summer, and Marge spotted a small farmhouse set back from the road." Better still would be, "When we were driving through Provence last summer, Marge spotted a small farmhouse set back from the road." Instead of a compound sentence with a conjunction, this complex construction is much more effective in holding the reader's interest. After this complex sentence finish up by making two more sentences.

"Since she read French, Marge told me they had rooms to let. We decided to stay for a week." There is no need to say, "We decided to stay. We stayed for a week." It is redundant. The sentence "We decided to stay for a week" makes more sense.

3.) Make Sure There is Subject-Verb Agreement.

"She work?" No, the correct subject/verb agreement is "She works." A singular subject takes a single verb. "We is?" It sounds terrible. "He don't write good?" Yikes! He sure doesn't, write *well*, that is.

"John and his wife goes?" Hopefully, they are going to take a grammar course.

Subject-verb agreement can be a big hurdle for ESL (English as a Second Language) students. My suggestion for these students, in addition to referring to the handbook, is to seek out help at the university's writing center. The service is free, and most centers require that you make an appointment first. Bring your rough drafts so you can work with the tutor to discover what mistakes you keep making and work to avoid them.

ESL students, of course, are not the only ones tripped up by subject-verb agreement. Many native-born speakers make errors, too. It is usually due to sloppiness, or the sad fact that grammar has never been hardwired in their use of English.

There is, however, one common cause for incorrect subject-verb agreement that afflicts even students with decent grammar—prepositional phrases. Read the following sentence:

"Michael and five of his fraternity brothers volunteer every Tuesday evening at the soup kitchen."

It sounds correct because you have a plural subject and a plural verb for the present tense.

But change the word "and," a conjunction, to the preposition "with" and everything changes.

"Michael, with five of his fraternity brothers, volunteers every Tuesday evening to volunteer at the soup kitchen."

Here's another example.

"The single mother with five children, two dogs, seven cats and two birds was evicted from the housing project."

A number of writers with good English skills might use "were" instead of "was" because the verb comes after a list of plural nouns, and the writers do not think. Those nouns, however, have no effect on the verb because they are not the sentence's subjects but part of a prepositional phrase beginning with "with." The subject is mother. Period. But if "with" is taken out, the subject becomes plural, and the verb becomes "were."

Prepositional phrases make even professional writers and editors slip up on subject-verb agreement.

Over the years I have even news stories and even editorials in some of the world's most respected newspapers guilty of this mistake.

In short, to avoid subject-verb agreement errors, always be cognizant of what the subject is and don't be fooled by prepositional phrases.

5.) Use the Right Cases for Personal Pronouns.

Another bête noire for editors and English professors alike is the mix-up of nominative and objective cases with personal pronouns. "I" "he/she," "they," and who" are nominative, subject pronouns. "Me," "him/her," "them," and "who" are objective. But how often do you hear lines like these?

"It's between him and I."

"Me and her went to a concert."

"Me and him are friends."

"Who did you see?"

The list goes on, especially in casual conversation. I even hear news-casters and announcers make these errors.

The problem with casual conversation, especially when you are trying to develop your writing voice, is that it often carries over into your writing. Students do it without thinking. The first sentence should be "It's between him and me," because "me" is the object of the preposition "between." Yes, prepositions have objects all of their own. The second sentence should be, "She and I went to the concert." The reason is that "I" is the nominative case. It's the doer, part of the compound subject. The third example, "Me and him are friends," is dead wrong on three counts. First, Standard English requires you to put yourself second—and always in the nominative case. Therefore, "He and I are friends."

And here's a final thought when it comes to proper grammar: Don't assume it is grammatically correct just because it sounds right. For example, you call up a close friend or family member. They answer, and you respond, "Hi, it's me." We all say, "It's me," which is wrong. Of course, if you go around saying, "It is I," you will sound pompous and pretentious. Still, when it comes to penning proper prose, Standard English rules apply.

Sometimes I long for the now derided days when students would diagram sentences on the blackboard (now whiteboard). A lot of teach-ers consider it an outmoded, Dark Ages practice that has nothing to do with the essence of writing. However, as stated earlier, grammar is hardwired into every language, and all writers must work within its rules to make their final drafts the best they can be in terms of thesis, voice, nuance, and style. Grammar is more than just a fresh coat of paint to make your prose look pretty. It's tightening the bolts so it will stand.

6.) Correct All Spelling Errors and Typos.

This goes without saying. However, it must be said. The worst thing that any new writer can do after he or she has worked long and hard on a paper is to let basic sloppiness rob that paper of its effect. In this age of computer spell checking, there is really no excuse for a paper rife with these kinds of mistakes. They can mean the difference between an A paper and a C paper. Spelling errors and typos cause your authority as a writer to take a hit. The reader figures that if you didn't care enough in this regard, your ideas and supporting research probably don't carry too much weight either.

Some final editing thoughts:

When editing your paper or another's, always adhere to the rule that good writing is clear and concise. Weed out unnecessary words to make the writing tighter and punchier. And make sure your paper follows the proper MLA format in terms of columns, headings, and page numbers required by your teacher.

Closing Thoughts

Perhaps some of you will go on to become professional writers. Most will choose other paths. Either way, remember that writing is a life skill, one that can only empower you.

The ability to articulate your thoughts clearly with logic, emotion and authority can only serve as a boon toward success whether you want to write an A+ paper for an economics class, history, or science class, a letter to your Congressman, or the next Great American Novel.

To those of you who have been smitten by the beauty and power of words and now want to be professional writers, I offer my best wishes and encouragement. Being a professional writer might not be the easiest life, but it can be the most rewarding, not financially in most cases, but in terms of personal enrichment and contribution. Robert Frost said it best in the last two lines of his poem "The Road Not Taken," almost an autobiographical take on his choice to become a writer:

"I took the one less traveled by,
And that has made all the difference."

Whatever road you choose, don't neglect the lessons learned here, even if sometimes you feel like throwing down your pen or walking away from your keyboard. Don't become discouraged by criticism from professors, editors, or even rejection slips if you choose the route of a professional writer. Just keep listening to that inner voice, the one telling you that you have something important to share because your voice counts. And always write with your head and your heart.

About the Author

James J. Lomuscio is a full-time professor in the Department of Writing, Linguistics, and Creative Process at Western Connecticut State University (WCSU). He also serves as a mentor in the university's Master of Fine Arts in Professional Writing program.

A journalist for more than 30 years, he has written for *Fairpress*, a Gannett newspaper, the *Connecticut* Post, the *New York Times* and served as editor of the *Westport News*, editor of *Westport Magazine* and editor of the online *WestportNow.com*. He is currently a special correspondent for the Stamford, CT *Advocate*. Over the years, the New England Press Association awarded him three first place writing awards for educational reporting, feature writing and spot news. He also won first place for spot news from The Society of Professional Journalists, and he is past president of the Connecticut Press Club.

In addition to teaching at Western, Mr. Lomuscio has taught rhetoric and advanced rhetoric at Sacred Heart University in Fairfield, CT, literature and composition at Norwalk Community College, composition at the University of Connecticut, and business writing at Albertus Magnus College. His previous book, *Village of the Dammed: The Fight for Open Space and the Flooding of a Connecticut Town,* was critically acclaimed and a 2006 finalist for the Connecticut Book Award in nonfiction. He lives in Weston, CT with his wife and two children.

135